Python Deep learning

Samuel Burns

Globaltech NTC

Python Deep learning

Develop your first Neural Network in Python Using TensorFlow, Keras, and PyTorch

Step-by-Step Tutorial for Beginners

Samuel Burns

Printed by Amazon Kindle Publishing

Editor: Paul Minani/GlobaltechNTC

Editorial Assistant: Zokolodni Sergey

E-Media Editor: Daniel Soler

Book Design: Rebecca F.

Collection: Step-by-Step Tutorial for Beginners

Deep learning: Develop your first Neural Network in Python Using TensorFlow, Keras, and PyTorch/ Globaltech NTC, Samuel Burns.

If you find any issues or you need the sample data files for this book, please contact us at globaltechntc@bk.ru

Book Objectives

The following are the objectives of this book:

- To help you understand deep learning in detail
- To help you know how to get started with deep learning in Python by setting up the coding environment.
- To help you transition from a deep learning Beginner to a Professional.
- To help you learn how to develop a complete and functional artificial neural network model in Python on your own.

Who this Book is for?

The author targets the following groups of people:

- Anybody who is a complete beginner to deep learning with Python
- Anybody in need of advancing their Python for deep learning skills.
- Professors, lecturers or tutors who are looking to find better ways to explain Deep Learning to their students in the simplest and easiest way.
- Students and academicians, especially those focusing on python programming, neural networks, machine learning, and deep learning.

What do you need for this Book?

You are required to have installed the following on your computer:

- Python 3.X
- TensorFlow
- Keras
- PyTorch

The Author guides you on how to install the rest of the Python libraries that are required for deep learning.

The author will guide you on how to install and configure the rest.

What is inside the book?

The content of this book is all about deep learning in Python. It has been grouped into chapters, with each chapter exploring a different feature of the deep learning libraries that can be used in Python programming language. The author has provided Python codes, each code performing a different task. Corresponding explanations have also been provided alongside each piece of code to help the reader understand the meaning of the various lines of the code. In addition to this, screenshots showing the output that each code should return have been given. The author has used a simple language to make it easy even for beginners to understand.

About the Author

Samuel Burns has a Ph.D. in Machine Learning and is an Artificial Intelligence developer, researcher, and educator as well as an Open Source Software developer. He has authored many papers as well as a number of popular software packages. Specialist in Data Mining and Security, Burns is an active machine learning researcher and regularly teaches courses and maintains resources for the data scientist.

Burn's research has pioneered developments in ensemble learning, outlier detection and profile discovery. He is involved in numerous international artificial intelligence and data mining research activities and conferences.

"I think people need to understand that deep learning is making a lot of things, behind-the-scenes, much better. Deep learning is already working in Google search, and in image search; it allows you to image search a term like "hug." "

Geoffrey Hinton

Introduction

Companies and businesses are generating huge amounts of data on a daily basis. This data is rich in terms of information. This information typically includes trends, patterns and relationships between various variables. Such information can help businesses in making better decisions. Businesses with such information can also enjoy a competitive advantage over those without. Deep learning is a great tool to help one in processing huge amounts of data. When the data is processed, the business will obtain information which is good for their growth. If the data is in the form of images, deep learning becomes the best tool for its processing. It involves the creation of artificial neural network machine learning models to extract trends, patterns and relationships from data. Such models work by imitating the way the human brain operates. Most of the available machines learning algorithms are only suitable for use on small datasets. The good thing with deep learning is that it can be used for processing huge amounts of data. Python is a great programming language for use in machine learning. Many libraries have been developed that can be used for creation of deep learning models. Most of these libraries are compatible with the Python programming language. This book is an excellent guide for you about deep learning with

Python. You will learn how to use the various deep learning libraries like TensorFlow, Keras and Pytorch in Python. The author guides from the initial steps of installing the libraries, creating deep learning models, training and testing them. Enjoy   reading!

Contents

Chapter 9- Creating Convolutional Neural Networks with PyTorch

Chapter 10- Creating Recurrent Neural Networks with PyTorch

Conclusion

Chapter 1- What is Deep Learning?

Deep learning is a branch of machine learning that is concerned with teaching computers to do what is natural to humans, that is, learning by example. Deep learning has empowered great projects like the driverless car, making it possible for the car to distinguish between lampposts and pedestrians, recognize stop signs, etc.

Deep learning is inspired by the structure of the human brain and how it operates. With deep learning, machines are able to perform tasks that require human intelligence to be performed. The machines learn from experience and acquire skills with the intervention by humans. Deep learning involves the use of artificial neural networks learn patterns, trends, and relations from large datasets.

Humans learn when they do a task repeatedly. Similarly, deep learning algorithms perform tasks repeatedly, while tweaking it in a bid to improve the outcome. With deep learning, computer models are able to perform classification tasks from text, images or sound. The deep learning models can provide a high level of accuracy, sometimes outperforming humans. Training of models is done using large sets of labeled data and neural networks with several layers.

Most methods for deep learning use neural networks, hence deep learning models are usually referred to as ***deep neural networks***.

The word **"deep"** refers to the number of hidden layers that a neural network has. Most neural networks have 2-3 hidden layers, but a deep neural network may have over 100 hidden layers. Training of such models involves the use of large sets of data. Neural network architectures with no need for manual intervention are then used to extract patterns from the data.

A good example of a deep neural network is the convolutional neural network **(CNN)**. CNN uses **2D** convolutional layers, which makes it good for processing of **2D** data like images. With CNN, there is no need for extracting features manually as you are not required to identify the features to be used for classifying images. CNNs directly extract features from images. The ability of deep learning models to extract features automatically makes them suitable for use in computer vision problems like object classification.

The CNNs rely on numerous layers to detect the features of an image. The complexity of the image features increases at every layer. In the first hidden layer, for example, the edges of the mages may be detected while the last layer may learn complex features in the image.

A good example of the application of deep learning is in fraud detection systems. Once it learns the normal procedures, any anomaly will be easily detected and classified as a potential for fraud.

Chapter 2- An Overview of Artificial Neural Networks

Neural networks form the core of deep learning. A neural network is a kind of network in which the nodes are seen as **"artificial neurons"**. The concept of the neural networks began in the **1980s**. The neural network of the human being is made up of a network of interconnected neurons for maintaining a high level of coordination to receive and then transmit messages to the spinal cord and the brain. In machine learning, such types of networks are referred to as **"Artificial Neural Networks (ANNs)"**.

The Artificial Neural Networks are made up of **"neurons"** which have been created artificially. These are then taught so that they can adapt to the cognitive skills of human beings. Some of the applications of ANNs are image recognition, soft sensors, voice recognition, time series predictions, and anomaly detection.

Neural networks are represented in the form of a mathematical model and they are mostly applied in machine learning. They are made up of neurons which are connected to each other, sending each other signal. A neuron receives signals until they exceed its threshold, and this is the time it fires, meaning that it forwards the signal to the next connected neuron in the network. The connections between the neurons can be done in the way we want, even to the same neuron, but the problem comes in when we need to train the network. This explains why restrictions have to be imposed in the creation of neural networks.

For the case of multi-layer perceptron, the neurons have been arranged into layers, and each neuron is allowed to pass signals only to the next neuron in the layer. The first layer in this is the input layer, while the last one is the output layer, and this will have the predicted values.

In artificial neural networks, learning refers to the process of modifying the bias and the weights that are fed to the network. Learning in neural networks is facilitated by training it, whereby a certain set of inputs are fed to the network while expecting a particular output, which is the target output.

This calls for adjusting the values for the weights and the biases so that they can give us the target output. The process of learning in artificial neural networks is similar to the concept of learning in human beings. The training is done repeatedly until we get the value of weights that give us the targeted outputs. After each training, normally referred to as an **epoch**, the weights are adjusted so that the error of the neural network can be reduced. This is done until the error is minimized completely.

Chapter 3- Exploring the Libraries

In this book, we will be using three libraries to build deep learning models. These libraries include the following:

- **TensorFlow**
- **Keras**
- **PyTorch**

TensorFlow

TensorFlow is a library/framework from Google used for the creation of deep learning models. TensorFlow relies on data-flow graphs for numerical computation. TensorFlow has made machine learning easy. It makes the processes of acquiring data, training machine learning models, making modifications and predicting future results easy.

The library was developed by Google's Brain team for use in large-scale machine learning. TensorFlow brings together machine learning and deep learning algorithms and models and it makes them much useful via a common metaphor. TensorFlow uses Python to give its users a front-end API that can be used for building applications, with the applications being executed in high-performance **C++**.

TensorFlow can be used for building, training and running deep neural networks for image recognition, handwritten digit classification, recurrent neural networks, word embedding, natural language processing, etc.

TensorFlow helps its users create dataflow graphs, which are structures describing the flow of data between graphs or processing nodes arranged in a series. Every node in the graph is a representation of a mathematical operation, and every edge connecting nodes is a representation of a tensor or multidimensional data array.

All of these are provided to the users via Python programming language. It is easy for one to learn Python, and provides an easy way of understanding how high-level abstractions can be put together. In TensorFlow, all tensors and nodes are Python objects, while the TensorFlow applications are Python applications.

However, math operations are not done in Python. The TensorFlow libraries used for transformations are written in high-performance **C++** binaries. The work of Python is to direct traffic between them and provides abstractions to connect them.

Applications developed in TensorFlow can be used on any convenient platform such as a cloud cluster, local machine, CPUS, GPUs, Android, and iOS devices. The models created in models can be used on a wide variety of devices for making predictions.

One of the greatest advantages of using TensorFlow is the abstraction it offers. Instead of being concerned with the low-level details regarding the implementation of algorithms, or looking for a proper way of channeling the output from a function as input to another function, the developer is allowed to focus on the entire logic concerning the application under development. TensorFlow then takes care of the rest of the details.

TensorFlow also provides developers with additional convenience when debugging their apps. It has the eager execution mode that allows one to evaluate every graph operation transparently and separately rather than having to make the whole graph as a single object then analyzing it at a go.

Keras

Keras is a deep learning library written in Python. It is used for the development of neural networks and it can run on top libraries such as Theano, TensorFlow, and CNTK. During its development, it was meant for fast experimentation.

The library was developed for human beings rather than machines, which has made it more users friendly. It gives a high priority to the user experience. The user is only expected to go through a small number of steps before completing any particular action.

Keras can also be extended with much ease. It is easy for us to add to it new modules and the existing modules come with many examples. The ability of Keras to allow the creation of new modules for expressiveness has made it a good library for advanced research.

PyTorch

PyTorch is a library based on Python developed to implement flexibility regarding the development of deep learning models. It has a workflow that is closely related to that of Numpy, a scientific computing library for Python.

The library was released in January of **2016** and many practitioners have adopted it for building neural networks because of its ease of use.

PyTorch relies on an Eager/Imperative paradigm. Each line of code that is needed for building the graph defines a component of the graph. Computations can be performed independently on these components itself, even before we are done with building the graph. This methodology is referred to as *define-by-run*.

PyTorch is well known for its dynamic computation graphs. It comes with a framework which we can use to build computation graphs instead of predefined graphs with specific functionalities. These graphs can be changed during runtime. Such a feature is useful when we don't know the amount of memory that will be needed for us to create a neural network.

Chapter 4- Installation and Setup

Installing TensorFlow

Now, you know the details of TensorFlow, hence you can install the library. TensorFlow comes with APIs for programming languages like C++, Haskell, Go, Java, Rust, and it comes with a third-party package for **R** known as *tensorflow*. We will be guiding you on how to install TensorFlow on Windows. On Windows, TensorFlow can be installed with **pip** or **Anaconda**.

The native pip will install the TensorFlow on your system without having to go through a virtual environment. However, note that installation of TensorFlow with pip may interfere with other Python installations on your system. However, the good thing is that you only have to run a single command and TensorFlow will be installed on your system. Also, when TensorFlow is installed via pip, users will be allowed to run the TensorFlow programs from the directory they want.

To install TensorFlow with Anaconda, you may have to create a virtual environment. However, within the Anaconda itself, it is recommended that you install TensorFlow via the `pip install` command rather than the `conda install` command.

Ensure that you have installed Python 3.5 and above on your Windows system. Python3 comes with a pip3 program which can be used for installation of TensorFlow. This means we should use the ***pip3 install*** command for installation purposes. The following command will help you install the CPU-only version for TensorFlow:

```
pip3 install --upgrade tensorflow
```

The command should be run from the command line.

If you need to install a GPU version for TensorFlow, run this command:

```
pip3 install --upgrade tensorflow-gpu
```

This will install TensorFlow on your Windows system.

You should verify whether the installation of TensorFlow was successful or not. Open the Python command prompt then run the following sequence of commands:

```
>>> import tensorflow as tf
>>> hello = tf.constant('Hello, this is TensorFlow!')
>>> ses = tf.Session()
>>> print(ses.run(hello))
```

The code should print the following:

```
Hello, this is TensorFlow!
```

If the code prints the above, then you have successfully installed TensorFlow on your Windows system.

Installing Keras

The process of installing Keras is easy as you only have to make a decision to use the preferred backend engine then install Keras just like any other Python library.

Keras runs on other libraries, which include TensorFlow, CNTK, or Theano, meaning that a backend engine is required for us to run Keras on it.

Keras is not meant for performing low-level operations, meaning that it has an advantage in modeling the higher-level layer, hiding the lower level details. The low-level operations rely depend on the backend, which includes the following libraries:

- **TensorFlow**- an open-source framework for symbolic tensor manipulation developed by Google.
- **Theano**- an open-source framework for symbolic tensor manipulation developed by LISA Lab, Université de Montréal.
- **CNTK**- an open-source toolkit developed by Microsoft for deep learning.

This means that we should have some of the above before installing the Keras library. TensorFlow forms the default backend library for the Keras library; hence I will recommend you ensure that you have installed it.

Once you have the Keras backend, you can install the Keras library by running the following command:

```
pip3 install keras
```

This should install the Keras library.

The default setting is that Keras will use TensorFlow as its backend. However, it is possible for you to change this to some other backend. This can be done using the *set* command. For example, to shift the backend from TensorFlow to Theano, we run the following command:

```
set "KERAS_BACKEND=theano"
```

You can then check whether Keras was successfully installed by running the *import* command as shown below:

```
import keras
```

Installing PyTorch

PyTorch can be installed on a number of various operating systems including Windows, Mac and the various Linux distributions.

On Windows, the installation of PyTorch is easy. To enjoy the PyTorch's ability to support CUDA, your Windows system must have NVIDIA GPU. PyTorch can be installed on Windows 7 and above, Windows 10 or above. You can also install it on Windows Server 2008 r2 or above.

Also, note that on Windows, PyTorch only supports Python 3.x, not Python 2.x.

In my case, I am using Python 3.5 and I need to install PyTorch via pip. I then run the following commands from the terminal of the operating system:

```
pip3 install
```

http://download.pytorch.org/whl/cpu/torch-0.4.1-cp35-cp35m-win_amd64.whl

```
pip3 install torchvision
```

The above is when your system has no CUDA support.

We can also install PyTorch through Anaconda in a non-CUDA Windows system. With Anaconda, a sandboxed environment will be created for this. You just have to run the following commands:

```
conda install pytorch-cpu -c pytorch

pip3 install torchvision
```

The two commands should setup PyTorch for you. You should now verify whether the installation was successful or not. On the Anaconda prompt, type **python** to access the Python terminal. You can then run the following statements from the opened Python terminal:

```
from __future__ import print_function
import torch
y = torch.rand(5, 3)
print(y)
```

Now that the code has run successfully, it is very clear that PyTorch is working correctly.

Chapter 5- TensorFlow Basics

DataFlow Graphs

In TensorFlow, computation is based on graphs. The graphs provide us with an alternative for solving mathematical problems. Consider the expression given below:

```
x = ( y+z ) * ( z+4 )
```

The above expression may also be expressed as follows:

```
p=y + z
q= z + 4
x= p * q
```

When represented as above, it becomes easy to express the expression in the form of a graph. Initially, we had a single expression but we now have two expressions. The two expressions can be performed in parallel. We can gain from this in terms of computation time. Such gains are very important in deep learning and big data applications, especially in Convolutional Neural Networks (CNNs) and Recurrent Neural Networks (RNNs) which are all complicated neural network architectures.

The goal of TensorFlow is to implement graphs and help in the computation of operations in parallel which will lead to efficiency gains. In TensorFlow, the graph nodes are known as **tensors** and they are simply multi-dimensional data arrays. The graph begins with the input layer where we find the input tensor. After the input layer, we get the hidden layer which has rectified linear units as an activation function.

Constants

In TensorFlow, we create constants using the function constant. This function constant has a signature given below:

```
constant(value, dtype=None, shape=None,
name='Const', verify_shape=False)
```

Where **value** is the actual constant value to be used for further computation, **dtype** is a data type parameter such as **int8/16**, **float32/64**, **shape** denotes optional dimensions, **name** is an optional name for the tensor while the last parameter is a Boolean indicating the verification of the shape of the values.

If you need constants with specific values in the training model, use the **constant object** as shown in the example given below:

```
k = tf.constant(5.2, name="x",
dtype=tf.float32)
```

Variables

In TensorFlow, variables refer to in-memory buffers with tensors that should be initialized explicitly and used in-graph to maintain state across the session. When the constructor is called, the variable is added to the computational graph.

Variables are mostly used when starting with training models, and they are used for holding and updating parameters. The initial value that is passed as the argument to the constructor represents the tensor or objects that is to be converted or returned as a tensor. This means that if we need to fill a variable with some predefined or random values that are to be used later in the training process and updated over the iterations, it can be defined in the following way:

```
m = tf.Variable(tf.zeros([1]), name="m")
```

In TensorFlow, variables can also be used in calculations whereby the variable is not trainable and it is definable as follows:

```
m = tf.Variable(tf.add(x, y),
trainable=False)
```

Sessions

For us to evaluate the nodes, the computational graph must be run within a session. The purpose of a session is to encapsulate the state and control of a TensorFlow runtime. If the session doesn't have parameters, it will use the default graph that was created in the current session; otherwise, the session class will accept the graph parameter, which is used in the session to be executed.

Let us run the **hello** code in TensorFlow:

```
import tensorflow as tf
h = tf.constant('Hello TensorFlow!')
s = tf.Session()
print(s.run(h))
```

The code returns the following:

```
Hello TensorFlow!
```

In the example given below, we are using all the terms defined above to calculate a very simple linear function in TensorFlow:

```
import tensorflow as tf
y = tf.constant(-2.0, name="y",
dtype=tf.float32)
a = tf.constant(6.0, name="a",
dtype=tf.float32)
b = tf.constant(13.0, name="b",
dtype=tf.float32)
```

```
z = tf.Variable(tf.add(tf.multiply(a, y), b))
init = tf.global_variables_initializer()
with tf.Session() as session:
    session.run(init)
    print session.run(z)
```

The code will return a **1** upon execution.

Placeholders

Suppose we are not aware of the value of array *y* during declaration phase of our TensorFlow problem, that is, before the stage for ***tf.Session()*** as ***ses***. In such a case, TensorFlow expects us to declare the basic structure of our data by use of **tf.placeholder** variable declaration. We can use it for **y** as shown below:

```
# creating TensorFlow variables
y = tf.placeholder(tf.float32, [None, 1],
name='y')
```

Since we are not providing any initialization in the declaration, we should notify TensorFlow of the data type of every element within the tensor. Our aim is to use *tf.float32*. Our second argument denotes the shape of the data to be injected in the variable. We need to use an array of size *(? x 1)*. Since we don't know the amount of data to supply to the array, we have used the **"?"**. The **placeholder** is ready to accept **None** argument for the size declaration. After that, we are now able to inject any amount of **1-**dimensional data we need into variable **y**.

Our program also expects a change in **ses.run(x,...)**.

This is shown below:

```
x_out = ses.run(x, feed_dict={y: np.arange(0,
10)[:, np.newaxis]})
```

Note that the argument **feed_dict** has been added to the command **ses.run(x,...)**. We have removed the mystery and we have specified what the variable y is expected to be, which is **1**-dimensional range between **0** and **10**. As the argument name suggests, **feed_dict**, the input we are to supply is a Python dictionary, and every key will be the placeholder name that we are going to fill.

Now you are done and you have implemented a graph in TensorFlow. You should have the following code:

```
import tensorflow as tf
import numpy as np
# Begin by creating a TensorFlow constant
const = tf.constant(2.0, name="const")
# create the TensorFlow variables
y = tf.Variable(2.0, name='y')
z = tf.Variable(1.0, name='z')
```

```python
# Let us create the operations
p = tf.add(y, z, name='p')
q = tf.add(z, const, name='q')
x = tf.multiply(p, q, name='x')
# creating a variable initialization
init_op = tf.global_variables_initializer()
# Launch the session
with tf.Session() as ses:
    # initialize the variables
    ses.run(init_op)
    # calculate the graph output
    x_out = ses.run(x)
    print("Variable x has a value of
{}".format(x_out))
# creating TensorFlow variables
y = tf.placeholder(tf.float32, [None, 1],
name='y')
x_out = ses.run(x, feed_dict={y: np.arange(0,
10)[:, np.newaxis]})
```

The code will return the following:

Variable x has a value of 9.0

Here is another example that shows how to multiply two variables in TensorFlow fashion. The **placeholder** has been used together with a feed mechanism via the run method of the session:

```
import tensorflow as tf
a = tf.placeholder(tf.float32, name="a")
b = tf.placeholder(tf.float32, name="b")
c = tf.multiply(a, b, name="c")
with tf.Session() as ses:
    print ses.run(c, feed_dict={a: 2.1, b: 3.0})
```

The code will return a 6.2999997 upon execution, which can be approximated to a 6.3.

Chapter 6- Deep Learning with TensorFlow

In this chapter, we will be demonstrating the process of training a neural network model in TensorFlow. This will be done using the API's estimator **DNNClassifier**.

This neural network will be trained using the MNIST dataset. The **MNIST** dataset serves as the *"hello world"* dataset for deep learning projects. This dataset is provided by the TensorFlow package. It has **28 /8 28 grayscale** image all with handwritten digits. The dataset has **55,000** training rows, **5,000** validation rows, and **10,000** testing rows.

Import the Data

First, let us import the libraries that we will be using:

```
import tensorflow as tf
import numpy as np
from keras.datasets import mnist
from keras.models import Sequential
from keras. layers import Dense
from keras.layers import Dropout
from keras.layers import Flatten
from keras.layers.convolutional import Conv2D
from keras.layers.convolutional import MaxPooling2D
```

```
from keras.optimizers import Adam
from keras. utils import np_utils
from PIL import Image
import numpy as np
import os
```

We will use the following code to load out dataset. The data can be imported by the use of the Keras library. You will see the progress of the data download:

```
(X_train, y_train), (X_test, y_test) =
mnist.load_data()
```

Next, it is time for us to reshape our data. Since we will use a convolutional neural network, we will reshape our data into batch, width, height and channels. The following code will help us to reshape the data:

```
X_train = X_train.reshape(X_train.shape[0],
X_train.shape[1], X_train.shape[2],
1).astype('float32')
X_test = X_test.reshape(X_test.shape[0],
X_test.shape[1], X_test.shape[2],
1).astype('float32')
```

It is possible for us to add our own images to both the training and test data.

This can be done as shown below:

```python
def load_images(image_label, image_directory,
features_data, label_data):
    files_list = os.listdir(image_directory)
    for file in files_list:
        image_file_name =
os.path.join(image_directory, file)
        if ".png" in image_file_name:
            img =
Image.open(image_file_name).convert("L")
            img = np.resize(img, (28,28,1))
            im2arr = np.array(img)
            im2arr =
im2arr.reshape(1,28,28,1)
            features_data =
np.append(features_data, im2arr, axis=0)
            label_data =
np.append(label_data, [image_label], axis=0)
    return features_data, label_data
```

The code will help us to load features and labels. Note that we have simply defined a function named *load_images()* taking in **4** parameters. It will list all the files that are available in the image directory. The function will check the format of the images, whether **png**. If you have **.jpg** files, then the **.png** will be changed to **.jpg**.

The images will then be loaded and converted into an array which is the same as the features data and an image array will be added to it. It will take an image label then add it to the ***label_data***.

Once all the images have been added to the folder or directory, the current dataset will return them back.

We now need to give the own images directories so that they may be loaded into existing dataset. This means that we will simply be loading the images into the training and the test sets:

```
X_train, y_train = load_images('1',
'F:/mnist', X_train, y_train)
X_test, y_test = load_images('1', 'F:/mnist',
X_test, y_test)
```

It is now time for us to normalize the data. The inputs will be normalized from 0-255 to 0-1:

```
X_train/=255
```

```
X_test/=255
```

We have labels, but they have not been categorized. It is now time for us to categorize them as shown below. It will be a one hot encodes:

```
total_classes = 10
y_train = np_utils.to_categorical(y_train,
total_classes)
y_test = np_utils.to_categorical(y_test,
total_classes)
```

It is now time for us to create the model. The following code demonstrates how to do this:

```
model = Sequential()
model.add(Conv2D(32, (5, 5),
input_shape=(X_train.shape[1],
X_train.shape[2], 1), activation='relu'))
model.add(MaxPooling2D(pool_size=(2, 2)))
model.add(Conv2D(32, (3, 3),
activation='relu'))
model.add(MaxPooling2D(pool_size=(2, 2)))
model.add(Dropout(0.5))
model.add(Flatten())
model.add(Dense(128, activation='relu'))
model.add(Dropout(0.5))
model.add(Dense(total_classes, activation='softmax'))
```

Note that dropouts have been added. These will ensure that our model doesn't suffer from over fitting. We can now compile our model:

```
model.compile(loss='categorical_crossentropy'
, optimizer=Adam(), metrics=['accuracy'])
```

Now that the model has been compiled without an error, it is time for us to train it. This can be done by executing the following command:

```
model.fit(X_train, y_train,
validation_data=(X_test, y_test), epochs=7,
batch_size=200)
```

Note that we have used only **7 epochs**. I have used 7 epochs as there are no significant improvements in the accuracy after the **7th epoch**.

 Downloading data from

https://www.dropbox.com/s/ttx8n7bdzzgp6np/mnist.npz?d

Or request it at globaltechntc@bk.ru

Our model is now ready.

The code gives the following result:

```
l=011493376/11490434
[==============================] - 0s
0us/step
11501568/11490434
[==============================] - 0s
0us/step
Train on 60000 samples, validate on 10000
samples
Epoch 1/7
60000/60000 [==============================]
- 32s 532us/step - loss: 0.4988 - acc: 0.8394
- val_loss: 0.0803 - val_acc: 0.9747
Epoch 2/7
60000/60000 [==============================]
- 30s 506us/step - loss: 0.1493 - acc: 0.9554
- val_loss: 0.0545 - val_acc: 0.9821
Epoch 3/7
60000/60000 [==============================]
- 27s 453us/step - loss: 0.1138 - acc: 0.9655
- val_loss: 0.0421 - val_acc: 0.9853
Epoch 4/7
60000/60000 [==============================]
- 26s 434us/step - loss: 0.0963 - acc: 0.9706
- val_loss: 0.0362 - val_acc: 0.9866
Epoch 5/7
60000/60000 [==============================]
- 27s 457us/step - loss: 0.0845 - acc: 0.9741
- val_loss: 0.0322 - val_acc: 0.9896
Epoch 6/7
60000/60000 [==============================]
- 33s 552us/step - loss: 0.0774 - acc: 0.9774
- val_loss: 0.0302 - val_acc: 0.9892
Epoch 7/7
60000/60000 [==============================]
- 29s 476us/step - loss: 0.0697 - acc: 0.9788
- val_loss: 0.0267 - val_acc: 0.9910
```

Chapter 7- Keras Basics

Learning Rate

Training a neural network or a deep learning model can be a difficult task. The standard algorithm used for training neural networks is known as **stochastic gradient descent**. It has been found that one can achieve an increased performance and a faster training on certain problems by use of a learning rate that is capable of changing over time.

Using an optimal learning rate for your stochastic gradient descent optimization procedure can reduce the training time and improve performance. The purpose of learning rate schedules is to adjust the learning rate during the training of a neural network. Let us discuss how these can be used with the Keras library:

Time-Based Learning Rate Schedule

The keras library comes with a time-based learning schedule built-in. The implementation of the stochastic gradient descent optimization algorithm in SGD class has an argument named **decay**.

We can use this argument in the time-based learning rate decay schedule equation as shown below:

```
LearningRate = LearningRate * 1/(1 + decay *
epoch)
```

When the value of the decay argument is **0**, which is also the default value, it means that there will be no effect on learning rate as shown below:

```
LearningRate = 0.1 * 1/(1 + 0.0 * 1)
LearningRate = 0.1
```

If you specify the decay argument, the learning rate will be decreased from the previous epoch by the fixed amount that is specified.

You can come up with a nice default schedule by setting your decay value as shown below:

```
Decay = LearningRate / Epochs
Decay = 0.1 / 100
Decay = 0.001
```

We need to create an example that demonstrates how to use the time-based learning rate schedule in Keras. We will use the Ionosphere binary classification problem.

The dataset can be obtained from the following URL:

https://www.dropbox.com/s/3cewwavkalc39l3/ionosphere.csv?dl=0 or you can request it at globaltechntc@bk.ru

Download the dataset and save it in a file named ***ionosphere.csv***. We will create a small neural network model with **one hidden layer and 34 neurons** and use the rectifier activation function. The output layer will have only one neuron and it will use the sigmoid activation function to generate probability-like values.

We will use a higher rate for the learning rate of stochastic gradient descent, **0.1**. A **decay** argument of **0.002 (0.1/50)** will be used and training will be done for **50 epochs**. Momentum is also good when using adaptive learning rate. Let us use a momentum of **0.8**. Ensure that you save the data above in the same directory as the file with this code:

```
import numpy
from tensorflow.python.keras.models import Sequential
from tensorflow.python.keras.layers import Dense
from pandas import read_csv
from sklearn.preprocessing import LabelEncoder
```

```python
from tensorflow.python.keras.optimizers
import SGD
seed = 7
numpy.random.seed(seed)
df = read_csv("ionosphere.csv", header=None)
dataset = df.values
X = dataset[:,0:34].astype(float)
Y = dataset[:,34]
encoder = LabelEncoder()
encoder.fit(Y)
Y = encoder.transform(Y)
mod = Sequential()
mod.add(Dense(34, input_dim=34,
kernel_initializer='normal',
activation='relu'))
mod.add(Dense(1, kernel_initializer='normal',
activation='sigmoid'))
epochs = 50
learning_rate = 0.1
decay_rate = learning_rate / epochs
momentum = 0.8
sgd = SGD(lr=learning_rate,
momentum=momentum, decay=decay_rate,
nesterov=False)
mod.compile(loss='binary_crossentropy',
optimizer=sgd, metrics=['accuracy'])
```

```
mod.fit(X, Y, validation_split=0.33,
epochs=epochs, batch_size=28, verbose=2)
```

After executing the code, it returns the following output:

```
Train on 235 samples, validate on 116 samples
Epoch 1/50
 - 0s - loss: 0.6885 - acc: 0.5915 -
val_loss: 0.6605 - val_acc: 0.7759
Epoch 2/50
 - 0s - loss: 0.6567 - acc: 0.7149 -
val_loss: 0.5738 - val_acc: 0.8190
Epoch 3/50
 - 0s - loss: 0.5909 - acc: 0.7702 -
val_loss: 0.4653 - val_acc: 0.8966
Epoch 4/50
 - 0s - loss: 0.5064 - acc: 0.8213 -
val_loss: 0.4256 - val_acc: 0.9483
Epoch 5/50
 - 0s - loss: 0.4190 - acc: 0.8468 -
val_loss: 0.3132 - val_acc: 0.9483
Epoch 6/50
 - 0s - loss: 0.3416 - acc: 0.8681 -
val_loss: 0.3045 - val_acc: 0.9224
Epoch 7/50
```

```
 - 0s - loss: 0.2996 - acc: 0.8766 -
val_loss: 0.2783 - val_acc: 0.9310
Epoch 8/50
 - 0s - loss: 0.2750 - acc: 0.8851 -
val_loss: 0.1860 - val_acc: 0.9569
Epoch 9/50
 - 0s - loss: 0.2242 - acc: 0.9149 -
val_loss: 0.2233 - val_acc: 0.9397
Epoch 10/50
 - 0s - loss: 0.2111 - acc: 0.9191 -
val_loss: 0.1896 - val_acc: 0.9655
Epoch 11/50
 - 0s - loss: 0.1872 - acc: 0.9319 -
val_loss: 0.1600 - val_acc: 0.9655
Epoch 12/50
 - 0s - loss: 0.1792 - acc: 0.9362 -
val_loss: 0.1069 - val_acc: 0.9741
Epoch 13/50
 - 0s - loss: 0.1756 - acc: 0.9277 -
val_loss: 0.1514 - val_acc: 0.9741
Epoch 14/50
 - 0s - loss: 0.1548 - acc: 0.9404 -
val_loss: 0.1525 - val_acc: 0.9569
Epoch 15/50
 - 0s - loss: 0.1532 - acc: 0.9447 -
val_loss: 0.1297 - val_acc: 0.9741
```

```
Epoch 16/50
 - 0s - loss: 0.1519 - acc: 0.9447 -
val_loss: 0.1949 - val_acc: 0.9310
Epoch 17/50
 - 0s - loss: 0.1357 - acc: 0.9574 -
val_loss: 0.1438 - val_acc: 0.9741
Epoch 18/50
 - 0s - loss: 0.1313 - acc: 0.9574 -
val_loss: 0.1211 - val_acc: 0.9828
Epoch 19/50
 - 0s - loss: 0.1276 - acc: 0.9617 -
val_loss: 0.1064 - val_acc: 0.9828
Epoch 20/50
 - 0s - loss: 0.1131 - acc: 0.9702 -
val_loss: 0.1309 - val_acc: 0.9828
Epoch 21/50
 - 0s - loss: 0.1095 - acc: 0.9617 -
val_loss: 0.0896 - val_acc: 0.9828
Epoch 22/50
 - 0s - loss: 0.1083 - acc: 0.9660 -
val_loss: 0.1242 - val_acc: 0.9828
Epoch 23/50
 - 0s - loss: 0.1060 - acc: 0.9617 -
val_loss: 0.1215 - val_acc: 0.9828
Epoch 24/50
```

```
 - 0s - loss: 0.1041 - acc: 0.9702 -
val_loss: 0.0961 - val_acc: 0.9828
Epoch 25/50
 - 0s - loss: 0.0962 - acc: 0.9745 -
val_loss: 0.1026 - val_acc: 0.9828
Epoch 26/50
 - 0s - loss: 0.0959 - acc: 0.9787 -
val_loss: 0.1102 - val_acc: 0.9828
Epoch 27/50
 - 0s - loss: 0.0911 - acc: 0.9745 -
val_loss: 0.0854 - val_acc: 0.9828
Epoch 28/50
 - 0s - loss: 0.0919 - acc: 0.9745 -
val_loss: 0.1126 - val_acc: 0.9828
Epoch 29/50
 - 0s - loss: 0.0876 - acc: 0.9787 -
val_loss: 0.0867 - val_acc: 0.9828
Epoch 30/50
 - 0s - loss: 0.0960 - acc: 0.9617 -
val_loss: 0.0821 - val_acc: 0.9828
Epoch 31/50
 - 0s - loss: 0.0878 - acc: 0.9745 -
val_loss: 0.1053 - val_acc: 0.9828
Epoch 32/50
 - 0s - loss: 0.0796 - acc: 0.9830 -
val_loss: 0.0901 - val_acc: 0.9828
```

```
Epoch 33/50
 - 0s - loss: 0.0757 - acc: 0.9830 -
val_loss: 0.0990 - val_acc: 0.9828
Epoch 34/50
 - 0s - loss: 0.0807 - acc: 0.9830 -
val_loss: 0.1277 - val_acc: 0.9655
Epoch 35/50
 - 0s - loss: 0.0853 - acc: 0.9660 -
val_loss: 0.0691 - val_acc: 0.9828
Epoch 36/50
 - 0s - loss: 0.0914 - acc: 0.9702 -
val_loss: 0.1031 - val_acc: 0.9828
Epoch 37/50
 - 0s - loss: 0.0743 - acc: 0.9830 -
val_loss: 0.1022 - val_acc: 0.9828
Epoch 38/50
 - 0s - loss: 0.0703 - acc: 0.9830 -
val_loss: 0.0813 - val_acc: 0.9828
Epoch 39/50
 - 0s - loss: 0.0709 - acc: 0.9830 -
val_loss: 0.0873 - val_acc: 0.9828
Epoch 40/50
 - 0s - loss: 0.0721 - acc: 0.9830 -
val_loss: 0.0863 - val_acc: 0.9828
Epoch 41/50
```

```
 - 0s - loss: 0.0647 - acc: 0.9830 -
val_loss: 0.0907 - val_acc: 0.9828
Epoch 42/50
 - 0s - loss: 0.0641 - acc: 0.9872 -
val_loss: 0.0931 - val_acc: 0.9828
Epoch 43/50
 - 0s - loss: 0.0645 - acc: 0.9830 -
val_loss: 0.0851 - val_acc: 0.9828
Epoch 44/50
 - 0s - loss: 0.0656 - acc: 0.9830 -
val_loss: 0.0789 - val_acc: 0.9828
Epoch 45/50
 - 0s - loss: 0.0628 - acc: 0.9830 -
val_loss: 0.0891 - val_acc: 0.9828
Epoch 46/50
 - 0s - loss: 0.0588 - acc: 0.9872 -
val_loss: 0.0755 - val_acc: 0.9828
Epoch 47/50
 - 0s - loss: 0.0584 - acc: 0.9872 -
val_loss: 0.0810 - val_acc: 0.9828
Epoch 48/50
 - 0s - loss: 0.0568 - acc: 0.9872 -
val_loss: 0.0819 - val_acc: 0.9828
Epoch 49/50
 - 0s - loss: 0.0571 - acc: 0.9872 -
val_loss: 0.0904 - val_acc: 0.9828
```

```
Epoch 50/50
 - 0s - loss: 0.0598 - acc: 0.9830 -
val_loss: 0.0790 - val_acc: 0.9828
```

The training has been done for a total of **50 epochs**. We have used **67%** of the dataset to train the model and **33%** of the dataset to test/validate the model. The code runs with an accuracy of **99.14%**, which is higher compared to a baseline of **95.69%** without the use of a learning rate decay or momentum.

Drop-Based Learning Rate Schedule

With this schedule, the learning rate is dropped systematically at certain times during the training. The method is implemented in such a way that the learning rate is dropped by half after each fixed number of epochs. For example, we can start with a learning rate of **0.1** then we drop it by **0.5** after every **10 epochs**. The first 10 epochs for which we train the model will use a learning rate of 0.1, the next **10 epochs** will use a learning rate of **0.05** and this continues.

This can be implemented in Keras by use of the LearningRateScheduler callback at the time of fitting of the model. With this callback, we can define a function that takes an epoch number as the argument and it, in turn, returns a learning rate to be used in the stochastic gradient descent. When this is used, the learning rate that is specified in the stochastic gradient descent will be ignored.

We will use the previous dataset of Ionosphere and create a network of a single hidden layer. We have created a new function named **step_decay()** to implement the following equation:

```
LearningRate = InitialLearningRate *
DropRate^floor(Epoch / EpochDrop)
```

The **InitialLearningRate** denotes the initial learning, which is a value such as 0.1, the **DropRate** denotes the amount by which we will modify the learning rate each time it is changed such as **0.5**, and the Epoch is the number of the current epoch while the **EpochDrop** denotes how often we will change the learning rate like 10.

The learning rate has been set to 0, which means that we will not be using it. However, if you need to use momentum, you can set it. The code for the drop-based learning rate schedule is given below:

```
import pandas
import numpy
import math
from pandas import read_csv
```

```python
from tensorflow.python.keras.models import
Sequential
from tensorflow.python.keras.optimizers
import SGD
from tensorflow.python.keras.layers import
Dense
from tensorflow.python.keras.callbacks import
LearningRateScheduler
from sklearn. preprocessing import
LabelEncoder
# the learning rate schedule
def step_decay(epoch):
    initial_lrate = 0.1
    drop = 0.5
    epochs_drop = 10.0
    lrate = initial_lrate * math.pow(drop,
math.floor((1+epoch)/epochs_drop))
    return lrate
seed = 7
numpy.random.seed(seed)
# load the dataset
dataframe = read_csv("ionosphere.csv ",
header=None)
dataset = dataframe.values
# create input and output variables
X = dataset[:,0:34].astype(float)
```

```python
Y = dataset[:,34]
encoder = LabelEncoder()
encoder.fit(Y)
Y = encoder.transform(Y)
# create the model
mod = Sequential()
mod.add(Dense(34, input_dim=34,
kernel_initializer='normal',
activation='relu'))
mod.add(Dense(1, kernel_initializer='normal',
activation='sigmoid'))
# Compile the model
sgd = SGD(lr=0.0, momentum=0.9, decay=0.0,
nesterov=False)
mod.compile(loss='binary_crossentropy',
optimizer=sgd, metrics=['accuracy'])
# the learning schedule callback
lrate = LearningRateScheduler(step_decay)
callbacks_list = [lrate]
# Fit a model
mod.fit(X, Y, validation_split=0.33,
epochs=30, batch_size=28,
callbacks=callbacks_list, verbose=2)
```

This time, the training has been done for **30 epochs**.

It returns the following upon execution:

```
Train on 235 samples, validate on 116 samples
Epoch 1/30
 - 0s - loss: 0.6892 - acc: 0.5957 -
val_loss: 0.6514 - val_acc: 0.9397
Epoch 2/30
 - 0s - loss: 0.6411 - acc: 0.7447 -
val_loss: 0.4974 - val_acc: 0.9483
Epoch 3/30
 - 0s - loss: 0.5387 - acc: 0.8085 -
val_loss: 0.4280 - val_acc: 0.9397
Epoch 4/30
 - 0s - loss: 0.3908 - acc: 0.8596 -
val_loss: 0.2803 - val_acc: 0.9310
Epoch 5/30
 - 0s - loss: 0.2853 - acc: 0.8894 -
val_loss: 0.1861 - val_acc: 0.9483
Epoch 6/30
 - 0s - loss: 0.2245 - acc: 0.9064 -
val_loss: 0.1506 - val_acc: 0.9483
Epoch 7/30
 - 0s - loss: 0.1910 - acc: 0.9319 -
val_loss: 0.1828 - val_acc: 0.9483
Epoch 8/30
```

```
  - 0s - loss: 0.1771 - acc: 0.9191 -
val_loss: 0.1197 - val_acc: 0.9741
Epoch 9/30
  - 0s - loss: 0.1536 - acc: 0.9489 -
val_loss: 0.0906 - val_acc: 0.9828
Epoch 10/30
  - 0s - loss: 0.1259 - acc: 0.9660 -
val_loss: 0.1438 - val_acc: 0.9569
Epoch 11/30
  - 0s - loss: 0.1107 - acc: 0.9745 -
val_loss: 0.0841 - val_acc: 0.9914
Epoch 12/30
  - 0s - loss: 0.1169 - acc: 0.9745 -
val_loss: 0.0872 - val_acc: 0.9828
Epoch 13/30
  - 0s - loss: 0.1092 - acc: 0.9574 -
val_loss: 0.0915 - val_acc: 0.9914
Epoch 14/30
  - 0s - loss: 0.0933 - acc: 0.9702 -
val_loss: 0.0940 - val_acc: 0.9914
Epoch 15/30
  - 0s - loss: 0.0907 - acc: 0.9745 -
val_loss: 0.0888 - val_acc: 0.9914
Epoch 16/30
  - 0s - loss: 0.0854 - acc: 0.9787 -
val_loss: 0.0877 - val_acc: 0.9914
```

```
Epoch 17/30
 - 0s - loss: 0.0814 - acc: 0.9787 -
val_loss: 0.0854 - val_acc: 0.9914
Epoch 18/30
 - 0s - loss: 0.0810 - acc: 0.9830 -
val_loss: 0.0719 - val_acc: 0.9914
Epoch 19/30
 - 0s - loss: 0.0763 - acc: 0.9787 -
val_loss: 0.0797 - val_acc: 0.9914
Epoch 20/30
 - 0s - loss: 0.0718 - acc: 0.9830 -
val_loss: 0.0758 - val_acc: 0.9914
Epoch 21/30
 - 0s - loss: 0.0719 - acc: 0.9830 -
val_loss: 0.0809 - val_acc: 0.9914
Epoch 22/30
 - 0s - loss: 0.0686 - acc: 0.9830 -
val_loss: 0.0697 - val_acc: 0.9914
Epoch 23/30
 - 0s - loss: 0.0677 - acc: 0.9830 -
val_loss: 0.0719 - val_acc: 0.9914
Epoch 24/30
 - 0s - loss: 0.0659 - acc: 0.9830 -
val_loss: 0.0755 - val_acc: 0.9914
Epoch 25/30
```

```
 - 0s - loss: 0.0650 - acc: 0.9830 -
val_loss: 0.0729 - val_acc: 0.9914
Epoch 26/30
 - 0s - loss: 0.0649 - acc: 0.9830 -
val_loss: 0.0717 - val_acc: 0.9914
Epoch 27/30
 - 0s - loss: 0.0651 - acc: 0.9830 -
val_loss: 0.0790 - val_acc: 0.9914
Epoch 28/30
 - 0s - loss: 0.0620 - acc: 0.9830 -
val_loss: 0.0681 - val_acc: 0.9914
Epoch 29/30
 - 0s - loss: 0.0629 - acc: 0.9830 -
val_loss: 0.0760 - val_acc: 0.9914
Epoch 30/30
 - 0s - loss: 0.0595 - acc: 0.9830 -
val_loss: 0.0695 - val_acc: 0.9914
```

The code gives me an accuracy of 99.14% upon execution on the test/validation dataset. This is also higher when compared to the baseline for the model.

Keras Optimizers

Each time that a neural network has finished passing a batch through a network and generated prediction results, it has to make a decision about what to do about the difference between the obtained results and the true values so that the weights to the network must be adjusted towards meeting a solution. This step is determined using an algorithm known as the *optimization algorithm*.

Keras comes with many optimization algorithms. Let us discuss how these can be used:

SGD

This stands for *Stochastic Gradient Descent* and it is a classical optimization algorithm. In this algorithm, the gradient of the network loss function is calculated in relation to every individual weight in the network. Every forward pass through the network leads to a particular parameterized loss function, and the gradients we have created are used for each weight, and then multiplied by a particular learning rate so as to move the weights in the direction that the gradient is pointing.

SGD can be said to be the simplest algorithm in terms of concepts and behavior. When this algorithm is given a small learning rate, it will follow the gradient on the cost surface. The new weights that are generated after every iteration are always better compared to the previous ones.

Due to the simplicity of the SGD algorithm, it has become very good for shallow networks. However, you should also note that the SGD algorithm converges a bit slowly compared to other more advanced algorithms that we have in Keras. It also has the least capability to escape the locally optimal traps that are available in cost surface. That is why the SGD algorithm is not commonly used in deep networks. It can be accessed from the following:

keras.optimizers.SGD

There are various parameters that are implemented by the SGD algorithm.

SGD with (Nesterov) Momentum

The Nesterov momentum is one of the parameters that made algorithms converge faster. The technique uses momentum. Momentum techniques work by introducing information from the previous steps to making a determination in the current step. This means that descent in an algorithm will not rely only on the current determination of the algorithm but also on some of the steps that it undertook previously.

Momentum has an advantage. It helps in handling a problem that is common when using the straight SGD, which is the problem of local minima traps. If the local minima are wide enough to push a gradient step back to itself, the SGD may get stuck. With momentum, the learner can jump and avoid the local minima. Momentum techniques also have another advantage in that optimizers are able to learn much quickly, which is achieved by selecting larger learning rates.

One of the best ways to apply iteration is for every iteration made by the learner, we create a vector of decaying average of the past steps that were taken by the algorithm, sum them with the vector of the current gradient, then take the direction of the summed vector.

The **nesterov momentum** varies this approach slightly for better results. It takes in a decayed average of the previous steps and the steps in that direction first. Next, we calculate the gradient from the new position by use of our data and we perform a correction. The weights are thus updated twice for every iteration, first using momentum and secondly using our gradient algorithm.

This explains why the **Nesterov momentum** is better compared to the simple momentum. It uses additional information, which is the gradient of the data at the uncorrected point.

By default, SGD doesn't use momentum. However, if you need to use momentum or **Nesterov momentum**, you can configure it as shown below:

keras.optimizers.SGD(momentum=0.01, nesterov=True)

Adagrad

This is an advanced machine learning technique that performs gradient descent using a variable learning rate. The node weights that were known to have large gradients are assigned large gradients, while node weights that were known to have small gradients are assigned small gradients.

This means that **Adagrad** is an effective SGD when used with a per-node learning rate scheduler that is built into the algorithm. Adagrad improves SGD by providing weights with learning rates that are historically accurate instead of relying on a single learning rate for all the nodes. Adagrad can be accessed as follows:

keras.optimizers.adagrad

Adadelta

This is a kind of **Adagrad** that relies on momentum techniq ues to handle the problem of monotonically decreasing learni ng rate. In **Adadelta**, the gradient update on every weight is a weighted sum of the current gradient and exponentially dec aying average composed of a limited number of the past grad ient updates. The gradient denominator, in this case, is not monotonically decreasing, hence the learning rate becomes more stable, and the overall algorithm becomes more robust.

In its first implementation, Adadelta required no learning rate parameter to be setup. However, the Keras library comes with a modified version of Adadelta with a defined learning rate that is in consistency with the other Keras optimization algorithms. We can adadelta in Keras as follows:

keras.optimizers.adadelta

RMSprop

This optimizer is a correction of Adagrad proposed independently of the adadelta optimizer. It is similar to Adadelta with the difference being that the learning rate has been divided further using an exponentially decaying average for all squared gradients, that is, global tuning value.

It is recommended that you leave the hyperparameters of this optimization algorithm in their default setting. It can be accessed as follows within the Keras library:

keras.optimizers.rmsprop

Adam (Adaptive Moment Estimation)

Just like **RMSprop** and **Adadelta**, it stores an exponentially decaying average of the past squared gradients. In addition to this, it stores an exponentially decaying average of decaying average of the past gradients, just like momentum.

Adam can be seen as a combination of RMSprop and momentum. It follows a path that is similar to the one of a ball with friction and momentum. Adam adds bias to the path followed by the algorithm towards a flat minimum on the error surface, with learning being made slow when moving on a large gradient.

Adam is currently amongst the popular optimization algorithms, which can be attributed to the fact that it provides a smart learning rate annealing as well as the momentum behaviors that it provides. It can be accessed as follows:

keras.optimizers.adam

AdaMax

Just like RMSprop and other optimization algorithms, this algorithm relies on an exponentially decaying weighted average obtained from the variance of the gradient in the formulation. However, there is no requirement for us to use the variance.

The variance is similar to the **L2** norm or second moment of the gradient. When compared to **Adam**, **Adamax** shows more robustness to gradient update noise and it has better numerical stability. It can be accessed as follows:

keras.optimizers.adamax

Nadam

Nadam is similar to Adam, but with **Nesterov momentum** rather than the ordinary momentum. The use of the Nesterov momentum in place of the ordinary momentum has a similar advantage as it is the case in SGD. This optimizer can be accessed as follows:

keras.optimizers.nadam

AMSgrad

This forms the recent proposal for improvement of the Adam optimizer algorithm. It was found that with some datasets, Adam doesn't converge to a globally optimal solution, but simple algorithms like SGD do.

It has been hypothesized that in some datasets such as those for image recognition, there are small, less informative gradients that are caused by the occasional large and more informative gradients. Adam comes with an inbuilt tendency to deprioritize more informative gradients since such is swallowed quickly by those weighting exponentially, making the algorithm to steer beyond the optimality point without exploring it sufficiently.

This algorithm has been found to perform very well on certain datasets, but it is yet to displace Adam due to its lack of verifiability when it comes to winning on general-purpose datasets. It can be accessed as follows:

keras.optimizers.adam(amsgrad=True)

Keras Metrics

With keras, you can list the metrics that you need to monitor when training your model. This can be done using the *metrics* argument then passing to it a list of function names to the *compile()* method on the model. Here is an example:

```
model.compile(...,metrics=['mse'])
```

The metrics that you list in this case can be names of the various Keras functions or string aliases of the functions.

The values of the metrics are recorded at the end of every epoch on the training dataset. If the validation dataset is provided, then the recorded metric will also be calculated for the validation dataset.

The metrics are reported in a verbose form in the history object which is returned after calling the *fit()* function. The metric function name is normally used as the key to the metric values. For metrics of validation dataset, we should use the **val_** prefix to the key.

Keras Regression Metrics

The following is a list of keras metrics that can be used for regression problems:

- Mean Squared Error- the mean_squared_error, MSE or mse
- Mean Absolute Error- the mean_absolute_error, MAE, mae
- Mean Absolute Percentage Error- the mean_absolute_percentage_error, MAPE, mape
- Cosine Proximity- the cosine_proximity, cosine

These can be tracked on a regression problem as demonstrated in the following code:

```
from tensorflow.python.keras.models import Sequential
from numpy import array
from matplotlib import pyplot
from tensorflow.python.keras.layers import Dense
# A sequence
```

```
X = array([0.1, 0.2, 0.3, 0.4, 0.5, 0.6, 0.7,
0.8, 0.9, 1.0])
# create a model
mod = Sequential()
mod.add(Dense(2, input_dim=1))
mod.add(Dense(1))
mod.compile(loss='mse', optimizer='adam',
metrics=['mse', 'mae', 'mape', 'cosine'])
# train the model
history = mod.fit(X, X, epochs=500,
batch_size=len(X), verbose=2)
# plot the metrics
pyplot.plot(history.history['mean_squared_err
or'])
pyplot.plot(history.history['mean_absolute_er
ror'])
pyplot.plot(history.history['mean_absolute_pe
rcentage_error'])
pyplot.plot(history.history['cosine_proximity
'])
pyplot.show()
```

The code should return the values of the metrics for every epoch.

Here is a section of the output from the code:

```
Epoch 175/500
 - 0s - loss: 0.1214 - mean_squared_error:
0.1214 - mean_absolute_error: 0.2890 -
mean_absolute_percentage_error: 66.3155 -
cosine_proximity: -1.0000e+00
Epoch 176/500
 - 0s - loss: 0.1202 - mean_squared_error:
0.1202 - mean_absolute_error: 0.2877 -
mean_absolute_percentage_error: 66.3311 -
cosine_proximity: -1.0000e+00
Epoch 177/500
 - 0s - loss: 0.1190 - mean_squared_error:
0.1190 - mean_absolute_error: 0.2864 -
mean_absolute_percentage_error: 66.3462 - co
```

Note that we specified by use of the string alias names and they were referenced as the key values on history object by use of their expanded function name.

The metrics could have been specified by use of their expanded function names as shown below:

```
, optimizer='adam',
metrics=['mean_squared_error',
'mean_absolute_error',
```

```
'mean_absolute_percentage_error',
'cosine_proximity'])
```

The function names can also be directly specified if they have been imported into the script:

```
from tensorflow.python.keras import metrics
model.compile(loss='mse', optimizer='adam',
metrics=[metrics.mean_squared_error,
metrics.mean_absolute_error,
metrics.mean_absolute_percentage_error,
metrics.cosine_proximity])
```

The loss functions can also be used as metrics. For example, to use the Mean squared Logarithmic Error loss function as a metric, you can do the following:

```
mod.compile(loss='mse', optimizer='adam',
metrics=['msle'])
```

Keras Classification Metrics

Below are the Keras metrics that can be used on classification problems:

- Binary Accuracy- binary_accuracy, acc
- Categorical Accuracy- categorical_accuracy, acc
- Sparse Categorical Accuracy- sparse_categorical_accuracy

- Top k Categorical Accuracy-
  top_k_categorical_accuracy . You should specify a k
  parameter.
- Sparse Top k Categorical Accuracy-
  sparse_top_k_categorical_accuracy. You should
  specify a K parameter.

Accuracy is a special metric. The **"acc"** metric can be
specified to report on accuracy regardless of the type of
problem in question. The code given below demonstrates a
binary classification problem and the use of the built-in
accuracy problem:

```python
from numpy import array
from tensorflow.python.keras.layers import
Dense
from tensorflow.python.keras.models import
Sequential
from matplotlib import pyplot
# prepare a sequence
X = array([0.1, 0.2, 0.3, 0.4, 0.5, 0.6, 0.7,
0.8, 0.9, 1.0])
y = array([0, 0, 0, 0, 0, 1, 1, 1, 1, 1])
# create a model
mod = Sequential()
mod.add(Dense(2, input_dim=1))
mod.add(Dense(1, activation='sigmoid'))
```

```
mod.compile(loss='binary_crossentropy',
optimizer='adam', metrics=['acc'])
# train the model
history = mod.fit(X, y, epochs=400,
batch_size=len(X), verbose=2)
# plot the metrics
pyplot.plot(history.history['acc'])
pyplot.show()
```

When the model is executed, it will report the accuracy
metric at the end of every training epoch. Here is a section of
the output from the code:

```
Epoch 1/400
 - 0s - loss: 0.7176 - acc: 0.5000
Epoch 2/400
 - 0s - loss: 0.7174 - acc: 0.5000
Epoch 3/400
 - 0s - loss: 0.7172 - acc: 0.5000
Epoch 4/400
 - 0s - loss: 0.7170 - acc: 0.5000
```

Custom Metrics

Keras allows us to specify our own metrics and specify the
name of the function in the list of functions for the

"metrics" argument when calling the ***compile()*** method on the model.

If you examine the code for any metric, you can get an idea about how to create your own custom metric.

For example, here is the code for the mean_square_error loss function metric in Keras:

```
def mean_squared_error(y_true, y_pred):
    return K.mean(K.square(y_pred - y_true),
axis=-1)
```

The K denotes the backend that is used by keras. One can use the standard math functions to calculate the metrics that they are interested in. The following example shows how to create a custom metric to calculate RMSE:

```
from tensorflow.python.keras import backend
 def rmse(y_true, y_pred):
    return
backend.sqrt(backend.mean(backend.square(y_pr
ed - y_true), axis=-1))
```

The code shows that it is similar to what we have for **MSE** but we have an addition of the ***sqrt()*** function to wrap the result.

We can try to use it in a regression example and see how it works:

```python
from numpy import array
from tensorflow.python.keras import backend
from tensorflow.python.keras.layers import Dense
from tensorflow.python.keras.models import Sequential
from matplotlib import pyplot


def rmse(y_true, y_pred):
    return
backend.sqrt(backend.mean(backend.square(y_pred - y_true), axis=-1))
 # A sequence
X = array([0.1, 0.2, 0.3, 0.4, 0.5, 0.6, 0.7, 0.8, 0.9, 1.0])
# create a model
mod = Sequential()
mod.add(Dense(2, input_dim=1, activation='relu'))
mod.add(Dense(1))
mod.compile(loss='mse', optimizer='adam', metrics=[rmse])
# train the model
```

```
history = mod.fit(X, X, epochs=500,
batch_size=len(X), verbose=2)
# plot the metrics
pyplot.plot(history.history['rmse'])
pyplot.show()
```

The training of the model has been done for 500 epochs. Here is a section of the output from the code:

```
Epoch 12/500
 - 0s - loss: 0.3734 - rmse: 0.5394
Epoch 13/500
 - 0s - loss: 0.3723 - rmse: 0.5384
Epoch 14/500
 - 0s - loss: 0.3713 - rmse: 0.5374
Epoch 15/500
 - 0s - loss: 0.3702 - rmse: 0.5364
Epoch 16/500
 - 0s - loss: 0.3691 - rmse: 0.5354
```

Keras Loss Functions

The training of deep learning neural networks is done using stochastic gradient descent optimization algorithm. During training, the error of any current state of the model should be assessed repeatedly. This requires one to use an error function, mostly referred to as a *loss function*. This function can be used for evaluating the loss made by a model so that the weights can be adjusted appropriately to reduce the loss during the next evaluation.

Neural networks map inputs to outputs and the chosen loss function should match the framing of a certain predictive modeling problem like regression or classification. Also, the output layer must also be configured well to match how the loss function has been configured.

Regression Loss Functions

In regression predictive modeling, we predict real-valued quantities. We will be discussing the loss functions that are appropriate for such problems.

We will be using the standard regression problem generator provided by the scikit-learn library in ***make_regression()*** problem. This function works by generating examples from a very simple regression problem with a particular number of input variables, statistical noise as well as other properties.

The function will be used for the definition of a problem with 20 input features, where 10 of these features will be relevant but the remaining 10 will not be relevant. We will randomly generate 1000 examples. We will use a fixed pseudorandom number generator to ensure that the code generates 800 examples each time it is executed. This is shown below:

```
# generate a regression dataset
X, y = make_regression(n_samples=800,
n_features=20, noise=0.1, random_state=1)
```

Neural networks exhibit a better performance when the goal is to scale real-valued input and output variables to a sensible range. In this problem, each input and target variables have a Gaussian distribution, making it desirable to standardize data in this case.

This can be achieved by use of the **StandardScaler** transform class provided by the scikit-learn library. If this was a real problem, we would have prepared the scaler on a standard dataset then apply it to the train and test sets. However, to make things simple, we will be scaling all our data together before we can split it into train and test sets.

```
# standardize the dataset
X = StandardScaler().fit_transform(X)
y =
StandardScaler().fit_transform(y.reshape(len(
y),1))[:,0]
```

Now that the data has been scaled, we can split it into the two sets:

```
# split data into train and test
```

```
n_train = 400
trainX, testX = X[:n_train, :], X[n_train:,
:]
trainy, testy = y[:n_train], y[n_train:]
```

We will define a small Multilayer Perceptron model to address this problem and give the basis as to why different loss functions should be explored.

The model will be expecting **20 features** as the input as we defined. Our model will consist of one hidden with a total of **25 nodes** and the rectified linear activation function will be used. The output layer will have only 1 node since only one real-value is to be predicted, and it will rely on a linear activation function.

```
# define the model
mod = Sequential()
mod.add(Dense(25, input_dim=20,
activation='relu',
kernel_initializer='he_uniform'))
mod.add(Dense(1, activation='linear'))
```

We now need to fit the model using stochastic gradient descent and a learning rate of 0.01 and momentum of 0.9, all being sensible default values.

We need to do the training for a total of 100n epochs and the test dataset will have to be evaluated at the end of every epoch. This will help in the generation of learning curves at the end of the process.

```
opt = SGD(lr=0.01, momentum=0.9)
mod.compile(loss='...', optimizer=opt)
# fit the model
history = mod.fit(trainX, trainy,
validation_data=(testX, testy), epochs=100,
verbose=0)
```

At this point, we have defined our model, hence we can go ahead and evaluate three loss functions that are appropriate for regression predictive modeling problems.

Mean Squared Error Loss

The MSE is the default loss used for regression problems.

Mathematically, it is the recommended loss function under inference framework of maximum likelihood if the target variable has a Gaussian distribution. This loss function should be evaluated first and changed only in cases where there is a good reason.

To calculate MSE, we get the average of the squared differences between predicted and actual values. The obtained result is always a positive value and with the perfect value being 0.0. Since there is square, it means that larger mistakes lead to big errors compared to smaller mistakes.

To use the mean squared error loss function in Keras, we specify the **"mse"** or **"mean_squared_error"** as the loss function during the time of compiling the model. This is shown below:

```
mod.compile(loss='mean_squared_error')
```

We recommend that you use one node for the output layer for the target variable and use a linear activation function:

```
mod.add(Dense(1, activation='linear'))
```

The following is a complete example demonstrating how to use MLP on a regression problem:

```
# mlp for regression and mse loss function
from sklearn.preprocessing import
StandardScaler
from sklearn.datasets import make_regression
from tensorflow.python.keras.models import
Sequential
from tensorflow.python.keras.optimizers
import SGD
from tensorflow.python.keras.layers import
Dense
```

```python
from matplotlib import pyplot
# generate a regression dataset
X, y = make_regression(n_samples=800,
n_features=20, noise=0.1, random_state=1)
# standardize the dataset
X = StandardScaler().fit_transform(X)
y =
StandardScaler().fit_transform(y.reshape(len(
y),1))[:,0]
# split the dataset into train and test sets
n_train = 400
trainX, testX = X[:n_train, :], X[n_train:,
:]
trainy, testy = y[:n_train], y[n_train:]
# define the model
mod = Sequential()
mod.add(Dense(25, input_dim=20,
activation='relu',
kernel_initializer='he_uniform'))
mod.add(Dense(1, activation='linear'))
opt = SGD(lr=0.01, momentum=0.9)
mod.compile(loss='mean_squared_error',
optimizer=opt)
# fit the model
```

```
history = mod.fit(trainX, trainy,
validation_data=(testX, testy), epochs=100,
verbose=0)
# evaluate model
train_mse = mod.evaluate(trainX, trainy,
verbose=0)
test_mse = mod.evaluate(testX, testy,
verbose=0)
print('Train: %.3f, Test: %.3f' % (train_mse,
test_mse))
# plot the loss during training
pyplot.title('Loss / Mean Squared Error')
pyplot.plot(history.history['loss'],
label='train')
pyplot.plot(history.history['val_loss'],
label='test')
pyplot.legend()
pyplot.show()
```

If the above model is executed, it will return the mean squared error for both the train and the test datasets.

Since the training algorithm is stochastic, the specific results may differ. That is why you execute the code for a number of times. In my case, I get the following:

```
Train: 0.003, Test: 0.009
```

This means that the model learned the problem and achieved an error of 0.003, to three decimal places.

Mean Squared Logarithmic Error Loss

We may encounter regression problems in which the target value is composed of a spread of values and when you need to predict a large value, you may not need to punish the model as heavily as the mean squared error.

Instead of this, you can begin by calculating the natural algorithm for each predicted value, then we determine the mean square error. This is referred to as the Mean Squared Logarithmic Error loss or MSLE in short. Its effect is relaxing the punished effect associated with large differences in large predicted values.

Since it is a measure of loss, it can be appropriate to use the model to predict **unscaled** quantities directly. We can create a demonstration of this loss function by use of a simple regression problem.

We can update our model to use a *mean_squared_logarithmic_error* loss function then we maintain the same configuration for the output layer. The mean square error will also be tracked as a metric during fitting of the model and use it as a metric to measure performance and plot a curve:

```
mod.compile(loss='mean_squared_logarithmic_er
ror', optimizer=opt, metrics=['mse'])
```

The following code demonstrates how we can use the MSLE loss function:

```
from sklearn.preprocessing import
StandardScaler
from sklearn.datasets import make_regression
from tensorflow.python.keras.models import
Sequential
from tensorflow.python.keras.optimizers
import SGD
from tensorflow.python.keras.layers import
Dense
from matplotlib import pyplot
# generate a regression dataset
X, y = make_regression(n_samples=800,
n_features=20, noise=0.1, random_state=1)
# standardize the dataset
X = StandardScaler().fit_transform(X)
y =
StandardScaler().fit_transform(y.reshape(len(
y),1))[:,0]
```

```python
# split the dataset into train and test sets
n_train = 400
trainX, testX = X[:n_train, :], X[n_train:,
:]
trainy, testy = y[:n_train], y[n_train:]
# define a model
mod = Sequential()
mod.add(Dense(25, input_dim=20,
activation='relu',
kernel_initializer='he_uniform'))
mod.add(Dense(1, activation='linear'))
opt = SGD(lr=0.01, momentum=0.9)
mod.compile(loss='mean_squared_logarithmic_er
ror', optimizer=opt, metrics=['mse'])
# fit the model
history = mod.fit(trainX, trainy,
validation_data=(testX, testy), epochs=100,
verbose=0)
# evaluate the model
_, train_mse = mod.evaluate(trainX, trainy,
verbose=0)
_, test_mse = mod.evaluate(testX, testy,
verbose=0)
print('Train: %.3f, Test: %.3f' % (train_mse,
test_mse))
```

The code will return the mean square error of the model on your train and test sets.

The training algorithm is stochastic in nature, which means that you may get varying results. Just run the code for a number of times.

From the obtained results, the model gave us a slightly worse MSE for both datasets, that is, the train and the test datasets. Due to this, it may not fit our problem since the target variable is a standard Gaussian. This is the result I got:

```
Train: 0.122, Test: 0.160
```

Mean Absolute Error Loss (MAE)

For a number of regression problems, the target variable may mostly have a Gaussian distribution, but it can have outliers, like values that are too far from the mean in terms of size.

The MAE loss is a good loss function for this case since it shows more robustness as far as outliers are concerned. To calculate it, we get the average absolute difference between the predicted and the actual values.

We can update the model to use the ***mean_absolute_error*** function but we maintain the same configuration for the output layer:

```
mod.compile(loss='mean_absolute_error',
optimizer=opt, metrics=['mse'])
```

The following example demonstrates how to use the mean absolute error as the loss function in a regression problem:

```
# mlp for regression with mae as the loss
function
from sklearn.preprocessing import
StandardScaler
from sklearn.datasets import make_regression
from tensorflow.python.keras.models import
Sequential
from tensorflow.python.keras.optimizers
import SGD
from tensorflow.python.keras.layers import
Dense
from matplotlib import pyplot
# generate a regression dataset
X, y = make_regression(n_samples=800,
n_features=20, noise=0.1, random_state=1)
# standardize the dataset
X = StandardScaler().fit_transform(X)
y =
StandardScaler().fit_transform(y.reshape(len(
y),1))[:,0]
```

```python
# split the dataset into train and test sets
n_train = 400
trainX, testX = X[:n_train, :], X[n_train:,
:]
trainy, testy = y[:n_train], y[n_train:]
# define the model
mod = Sequential()
mod.add(Dense(25, input_dim=20,
activation='relu',
kernel_initializer='he_uniform'))
mod.add(Dense(1, activation='linear'))
opt = SGD(lr=0.01, momentum=0.9)
mod.compile(loss='mean_absolute_error',
optimizer=opt, metrics=['mse'])
# fit the model
history = mod.fit(trainX, trainy,
validation_data=(testX, testy), epochs=100,
verbose=0)
# evaluate the model
_, train_mse = mod.evaluate(trainX, trainy,
verbose=0)
_, test_mse = mod.evaluate(testX, testy,
verbose=0)
print('Train: %.3f, Test: %.3f' % (train_mse,
test_mse))
```

When the model is executed, it will return the mean square error for both the train and the test datasets. Again, due to the stochastic nature of the algorithm, the results may differ; hence you should execute the model for a number of times. The model has learned the problem to achieve an error that is almost zero:

```
Train: 0.008, Test: 0.011
```

Binary Classification Loss Functions

Binary classification refers to the predictive modeling problems in which examples are assigned one of two labels.

Problems in this case are framed as predicting whether a value is a `0` or `1` and we implement it as predicting the probability of a value belongs to the class value **1**. We will be discussing the loss functions that are appropriate for the binary classification predictive modeling problems. Examples will be generated from circles test problem of the scikit-learn library. `800` **samples** will be generated and a statistical noise of `10%` will be added.

```
# generate the circles
X, y = make_circles(n_samples=800, noise=0.1,
random_state=1)
```

We can now split the dataset into train and test sets:

```
# split the dataset into train and test sets
n_train = 400
trainX, testX = X[:n_train, :], X[n_train:,
:]
trainy, testy = y[:n_train], y[n_train:]
```

Let us create a simple MLP to address the problem:

```
# define the model
Mod = Sequential()
mod.add(Dense(50, input_dim=2,
activation='relu',
kernel_initializer='he_uniform'))
mod.add(Dense(1, activation='...'))
```

We will use stochastic descent gradient to fit the model and use a default learning rate of 0.01 and a momentum of 0.9:

```
opt = SGD(lr=0.01, momentum=0.9)
mod.compile(loss='...', optimizer=opt,
metrics=['accuracy'])
```

The model will be run for **150 epochs** then we will evaluate it against loss and accuracy at the end of every epoch:

```
# fit the model
```

```
history = model.fit(trainX, trainy,
validation_data=(testX, testy), epochs=150,
verbose=0)
```

The basis for the problem has been obtained. Let us explore how to use loss functions on it.

Binary Cross-Entropy Loss

Cross-entropy forms the default loss function for use in binary classification problems. It should be used in classification problems where the target values belong to the set {0,1}.

To use cross-entropy in Keras library, we can specify the **_binary_crossentropy_** parameter during the time of compiling the model as shown below:

```
mod.compile(loss='binary_crossentropy',
optimizer=opt, metrics=['accuracy'])
```

With this function, the output layer should be configured with only a single layer then we use a sigmoid activation function for the purpose of predicting the probability of class 1.

```
mod.add(Dense(1, activation='sigmoid'))
```

Here is the complete example showing how to use **MLP** with cross-entropy loss for two circles binary classification problem:

```python
# mlp for circles problem with a cross
entropy loss
from sklearn.datasets import make_circles
from tensorflow.python.keras.layers import
Dense
from tensorflow.python.keras.models import
Sequential
from matplotlib import pyplot
from tensorflow.python.keras.optimizers
import SGD
# generate a 2d classification dataset
X, y = make_circles(n_samples=800, noise=0.1,
random_state=1)
# split the dataset into train and test sets
n_train = 400
trainX, testX = X[:n_train, :], X[n_train:,
:]
trainy, testy = y[:n_train], y[n_train:]
# define the model
mod = Sequential()
```

```python
mod.add(Dense(50, input_dim=2,
activation='relu',
kernel_initializer='he_uniform'))
mod.add(Dense(1, activation='sigmoid'))
opt = SGD(lr=0.01, momentum=0.9)
mod.compile(loss='binary_crossentropy',
optimizer=opt, metrics=['accuracy'])
# fit the model
history = mod.fit(trainX, trainy,
validation_data=(testX, testy), epochs=150,
verbose=0)
# evaluate model
_, train_acc = mod.evaluate(trainX, trainy,
verbose=0)
_, test_acc = mod.evaluate(testX, testy,
verbose=0)
print('Train: %.3f, Test: %.3f' % (train_acc,
test_acc))
```

The model returns the classification accuracy for both the train and test sets when executed:

```
Train: 0.820, Test: 0.787
```

The above shows that the model was able to attain an accuracy of 82% on the train set and an accuracy of 78% on the test set. This shows that our model is neither over nor underfit.

Hinge Loss

This is an alternative to the cross-entropy when it comes to binary classification problems. It was developed to be used for **Support Vector Machines** (SVM).

This loss function should be used for binary classification problems in which the target values belong to the set {-1,1}. We should first modify the variable to have these values in the set:

```
# change the y from {0,1} to {-1,1}
y[where(y == 0)] = -1
```

To use the hinge loss function, we need to specify the parameter *hinge* during the compile time of the model:

```
mod.compile(loss='hinge', optimizer=opt,
metrics=['accuracy'])
```

The output layer of the model should be configured to have a single node and use the hyperbolic tangent activation function as it can output a single value that is within the range of [-1,1].

```
mod.add(Dense(1, activation='tanh'))
```

The complete MLP code should be as follows:

```python
# mlp for circles problem with a hinge loss
from sklearn.datasets import make_circles
from tensorflow.python.keras.layers import Dense
from tensorflow.python.keras.models import Sequential
from tensorflow.python.keras.optimizers import SGD
from numpy import where
from matplotlib import pyplot


# generate a 2d classification dataset
X, y = make_circles(n_samples=800, noise=0.1, random_state=1)
# change the y from {0,1} to {-1,1}
y[where(y == 0)] = -1
# split the dataset into train and test sets
n_train = 400
trainX, testX = X[:n_train, :], X[n_train:, :]
trainy, testy = y[:n_train], y[n_train:]
# define the model
mod = Sequential()
```

```
mod.add(Dense(50, input_dim=2,
activation='relu',
kernel_initializer='he_uniform'))
mod.add(Dense(1, activation='tanh'))
opt = SGD(lr=0.01, momentum=0.9)
mod.compile(loss='hinge', optimizer=opt,
metrics=['accuracy'])
# fit the model
history = mod.fit(trainX, trainy,
validation_data=(testX, testy), epochs=200,
verbose=0)
# evaluate the model
_, train_acc = mod.evaluate(trainX, trainy,
verbose=0)
_, test_acc = mod.evaluate(testX, testy,
verbose=0)
print('Train: %.3f, Test: %.3f' % (train_acc,
test_acc))
```

The model will return the classification accuracy of the model on both the test and train sets. Since the algorithm is stochastic, the results may differ, hence you should consider executing the model for a number of times. The model is less accurate compared to when using the cross-entropy, with the accuracy on both the training and test sets being less than 80%:

```
Train: 0.395, Test: 0.357
```

Squared Hinge Loss

The following code shows how we can apply this loss function:

```python
# mlp for circles problem with a squared
hinge loss
from sklearn.datasets import make_circles
from tensorflow.python.keras.layers import
Dense
from tensorflow.python.keras.models import
Sequential
from matplotlib import pyplot
from tensorflow.python.keras.optimizers
import SGD
from numpy import where
# generate a 2d classification dataset
X, y = make_circles(n_samples=800, noise=0.1,
random_state=1)
# change the y from {0,1} to {-1,1}
y[where(y == 0)] = -1
# split the dataset into train and test sets
n_train = 400
```

```python
trainX, testX = X[:n_train, :], X[n_train:,
:]
trainy, testy = y[:n_train], y[n_train:]
# define the model
mod = Sequential()
mod.add(Dense(50, input_dim=2,
activation='relu',
kernel_initializer='he_uniform'))
mod.add(Dense(1, activation='tanh'))
opt = SGD(lr=0.01, momentum=0.9)
mod.compile(loss='squared_hinge',
optimizer=opt, metrics=['accuracy'])
# fit the model
history = mod.fit(trainX, trainy,
validation_data=(testX, testy), epochs=150,
verbose=0)
# evaluate the model
_, train_acc = mod.evaluate(trainX, trainy,
verbose=0)
_, test_acc = mod.evaluate(testX, testy,
verbose=0)
print('Train: %.3f, Test: %.3f' % (train_acc,
test_acc))
```

The model returns an accuracy that is below **70%** on both the train and test sets as shown below:

```
Train: 0.318, Test: 0.275
```

Chapter 8- PyTorch Basics

Computational Graphs

Deep learning is most implemented programmatically via computational graphs. It is simply a set of calculations known as nodes, with the nodes being connected in a directional ordering of computation. What this means is that some of the nodes on the graph rely on other nodes for their input, and these nodes, in turn, pass their outputs to serve as inputs to other nodes.

In such graphs, each node can be treated as an independently working piece of code. This way, performance optimizations can be done to implement calculations like threading and multiple **processing/parallelism**. All frameworks for deep learning like TensorFlow and Theano work by the construction of such graphs through which can be able to perform neural network operations.

Tensors

Tensors are data structures that look like matrices and they are very critical components for efficient computation in deep learning. GPUs (Graphical Processing Units) are very effective when it comes to performing operations between tensors, and this has become very popular in deep learning.

There are various ways through which we can declare tensors in PyTorch. Let us discuss them:

```
import torch
x = torch.Tensor(2, 4)
```

The above code will generate a tensor of size (2, 4), that is, 2 **rows** and 4 **columns**. We can display it by running the print statement:

```
print(x)
```

```
>>> import torch
>>> x = torch.Tensor(2, 4)
>>> print(x)
tensor([[1.6009e-19, 4.4721e+21, 6.2625e+22, 4.7428e+30],
        [1.4586e-19, 6.7967e-33, 0.0000e+00, 1.4013e-45]])
>>>
```

We can also create a tensor of random float values as shown below:

```
x = torch.rand(2, 4)
```

We can perform mathematical operations on tensors:

```
x = torch.ones(2,4)
y = torch.ones(2,4) * 2
x + y
```

This will print the following:

```
>>> x = torch.ones(2,4)
>>> y = torch.ones(2,4) * 2
>>> x + y
tensor([[3., 3., 3., 3.],
        [3., 3., 3., 3.]])
>>>
```

Autograd in PyTorch

Deep learning libraries should provide a mechanism for calculating error gradients and propagating them backwards in the computational graph. PyTorch provides such a mechanism which is given the name **autograd**. The mechanism is intuitive and easily accessible. The main component for this system is the *Variable* class. We can import the Variable class as shown below:

```
from torch.autograd import Variable
```

We can then create a variable as shown below:

```
var_x = Variable(torch.randn((4,3)))
```

Building a Neural Network

We need to demonstrate how to build a neural network in PyTorch.

We will be creating a 4-layer neural network, fully connected then use it to analyze the **MNIST** dataset. The network will classify the handwritten digits of this datasets. The network will have two hidden layers.

The input layer will have **28 x 28 (=784) greyscale pixels** which make up the MNIST dataset. Once the data is received at the input layer, it will be propagated through the two hidden layers, each having **200 nodes**. The nodes will use the **ReLU** activation function. The output layer will have **10 nodes** which represent the 10 classes to which each digit can belong to. A **softmax** output layer will be used for the purpose of performing the classification.

The Neural Network Class

The creation of neural networks in PyTorch is done via the ***nn.Module***. This is a base class, and we use inheritance to access it. After the import, we will be able to use all the functionality of ***nn. Module*** base class, but we will still have the overwriting capabilities of the base class for forwarding pass/ model construction through the network. Let us explain this using the code:

```python
import torch.nn.functional as F
import torch.nn as nn
class NeuralNet(nn.Module):
    def __init__(self):
        super(NeuralNet, self).__init__()
```

```
self.fc1 = nn.Linear(28 * 28, 200)
self.fc2 = nn.Linear(200, 200)
self.fc3 = nn.Linear(200, 10)
```

We import **nn.Module** class through inheritance. In the first line of our class initialization, that is, **def __init__(self)**: we have the **super()** function. This will create an instance of the base class, that is, **nn.Module**. The next three lines have then been used to create fully connected layers of the neural network. The **nn.Linear** object represents a fully connected. The first argument in this definition denotes the number of nodes in the layer. The next argument denotes the number of nodes in the layer $l + 1$. The first layer will take **28 * 28** input pixels and it will connect to the first **200 nodes** hidden layer. We then have **200** to **200** hidden layers then a connection between the hidden layer and the output layer with a total of **10 nodes**.

At this point, we have created a skeleton of our network architecture. It is now time for us to define how the data will flow through the network. This should be done by adding the **forward()** method to our class which will overwrite the dummy method in our base class, and this should be defined for every network. This can be done as follows:

```
def forward(self, y):
    y = F.relu(self.fc1(y))
```

```
y = F.relu(self.fc2(y))
y = self.fc3(y)
return F.log_softmax(y)
```

In the *forward()* method defined above, we have passed the input data **y** to be the primary argument. This has then been fed into the first fully connected layer, that is, *self.fc1(y)*. *A ReLU* activation function has then been applied to the nodes in the layer via *F.relu()*. The network is hierarchical in nature, hence we have added y at every stage so that it can be fed into the next layer. This has been through the three fully connected layers, except the last one, where we have used a *log softmax* activation function rather than **ReLU**. This, when combined with negative log likelihood loss function returns a multi-class cross entropy based loss function that will be used for training the network.

Next, we need to create an instance of our network architecture:

```
net = NeuralNet()

print(net)
```

The instance has been given the name *net* as shown above. We have then used the *print()* function to print out the instance of our *NeuralNet* class.

It returns the following:

```
NeuralNet(
    (fc1): Linear(in_features=784, out_features=200, bias=True)
    (fc2): Linear(in_features=200, out_features=200, bias=True)
    (fc3): Linear(in_features=200, out_features=10, bias=True)
)
```

The above output tells us more about the structure of our neural network.

Training

It is now time for us to train the network. We should begin by setting up an optimizer and a loss criterion. First, run the following import statement:

```
import torch.optim as optim
```

Then add the following code:

```
# Lets first create a stochastic gradient
descent optimizer
optimizer = optim.SGD(net.parameters(),
lr=0.01, momentum=0.9)
# Then we create a loss function
criterion = nn.NLLLoss()
```

We first created a stochastic gradient descent optimizer and specified the learning rate of 0.01 and momentum of **0.9**. We also need to supply all the network parameters to the optimizer. The ***parameters ()*** method provides us with an easy way of passing on these parameters. This method can be found from the **nn. *Module*** class that can be inherited from in NeuralNet class.

We then set the loss criterion to be a negative log likelihood loss. When this is combined with the log **softmax** output from the neural network, we get an equivalent cross entropy loss for the 10 classification classes.

During the training of the network, we will extract data from data loader object that comes included in the utilities module of PyTorch. The data loader will supply the input in batches then target data that will be supplied to the network and the loss function respectively. The training code is given below:

```
# execute the main training loop
for epoch in range(epochs):
    for batch_idx, (data, target) in
enumerate(train_loader):
        data, target = Variable(data),
Variable(target)
        # resize the data from (batch_size,
1, 28, 28) to (batch_size, 28*28)
        data = data.view(-1, 28*28)
        optimizer.zero_grad()
        net_out = net(data)
        loss = criterion(net_out, target)
```

```
loss.backward()
optimizer.step()
if batch_idx % log_interval == 0:
    print('Training Epoch: {} [{}/{}
({:.0f}%)]\tLoss: {:.6f}'.format(
            epoch, batch_idx *
len(data), len(train_loader.dataset),
                100. * batch_idx /
len(train_loader), loss.data[0]))
```

The outer training loop denotes the number of epochs, while the inner training loop will run through the whole training set in batch sizes that are specified as **batch_size** in the code. The data and target have then been converted into PyTorch variables. The **torchvision** package comes with the **MNIST** dataset will have a size of *(batch_size, 1, 28, 28)* after it is extracted from the data loader. Such a 4D sensor is more suitable for convolutional neural network architecture than our fully connected neural network. This is why we should flatten our (**1, 28, 28**) data into a single dimension of **28 x 28 = 784** input nodes.

The work of the *.view()* function is to operate on the PyTorch variables and reshape them appropriately. A notation of **-1** can also be used in the definition. If we use *data.view(-1, 28*28)*, it means that the second dimension has to be equal to **28 * 28**, but the first dimension has to be calculated from the size of the original data variable. Practically, it means that the data will be of size *(batch_size, 784)*. A batch of input data can be passed like this into the network and PyTorch will be able to efficiently perform all the necessary operations on the tensors.

We have then run the ***optimizer.zero_grad()*** which resets or zeroes all the gradients in the model, meaning that it will be ready for the next back propagation pass. In other deep learning libraries, this process is done implicitly but PyTorch requires you to do it explicitly. Here are the two lines:

```
n_out = net(data)
loss = criterion(n_out, target)
```

The first line allows us to pass the input data batch into the model. What this does is that it calls the *forward()* method in the Net class. After running the above line, the variable *n_out* will store the output from the log **softmax** of the neural network for the provided data batch. This is one of the best things with PyTorch as it allows you to activate any normal Python debugger that you use usually and get an idea of what is happening in the network instantly. This is not the case with other deep learning libraries like Keras and TensorFlow which expect elaborate debugging sessions to be setup before you can know what is really happening in the network.

In the next line, we get the negative log likelihood loss between the output of the network and the target batch data. The next two lines of code are as follows:

```
loss.backward()
optimizer.step()
```

The first line given above will run a back-propagation operation from loss variable then backwards through our network. In this case, no argument has been passed to the *.backward()* function. When calling the *.backward()* operation on scalar variables, they don't expect us to pass an argument to them. However, tensors expect us to pass a matching sized tensor argument to the *.backward()* function.

In the second line above, we are telling PyTorch above to run a gradient descent step depending on the gradients that were calculated during the *.backward()* operation.

Finally, we have printed out some results after attaining a specified number of iterations.

This is shown below:

```
if batch_idx % log_interval == 0:
    print('Train Epoch: {} [{}/{}
({:.0f}%)]\tLoss: {:.6f}'.format(
                    epoch, batch_idx *
len(data), len(train_loader.dataset),
                    100. * batch_idx /
len(train_loader), loss.data[0]))
```

The print function will show us the progress through the epochs and give the network loss at that point in training. You should note the way you access the loss, you access Variable .data property, which will be an array of single value. The scalar los can be accessed by executing **loss.data[0]**.

After training the network for **10 epochs**, you will get a loss value whose value is below a magnitude of **0.05**.

Testing

The following code can help us to test the trained network on the MNIST dataset:

```
# Execute a test loop
test_loss = 0
correct = 0
```

```python
for data, target in test_loader:
    data, target = Variable(data,
volatile=True), Variable(target)
    data = data.view(-1, 28 * 28)
    n_out = net(data)
    # Get the sum of batch loss
    test_loss += criterion(n_out,
target).data[0]
    pred = n_out.data.max(1)[1]
# obtain the index of max log-probability
    correct += pred.eq(target.data).sum()
test_loss /= len(test_loader.dataset)
print('\nTest set: Average loss: {:.4f},
Accuracy: {}/{} ({:.0f}%)\n'.format(
        test_loss, correct,
len(test_loader.dataset),
        100. * correct /
len(test_loader.dataset)))
```

The above loop is similar to our previous training loop up too where we have the **test_loss** line. In this line, we are extracting the loss of the network using **.data[o]** property, and this has been done in one line. In the **pred** line, we have used **data.max(1)**, the **.max()** function is able to return the index of the maximum value in a particular dimension of a tensor. The neural network will then give us an output of size **(batch_size, 10)**, where every value of the 10-length second dimension will be a log probability assigned by the network to each output class. This simply means that it is the log probability showing whether the provided image is an image that is between **0** and **9**.

The value with the highest log probability will be the digit the network considers to be the most probable when given the input image, which forms the best prediction of the class from the network. The function **.max(1)** will determine the maximum value in the second dimension. It will then return the maximum value that is found as well as the index at which this value was found to be at. This means its size is **(batch_size, 2)**, but we are interested in the index in which the maximum value is located, hence the values can be accessed by calling **.max(1)[1]**.

At this point, we have the prediction of our neural network for every sample in the batch already determined; hence this can be compared with the actual target class from the training data. This will involve counting the number of times that our neural network managed to get it right. This can be done by calling the **PyTorch .eq()** function, which works by comparing the values in two sensors. If these values match, it returns a 1. If the values don't match, it returns a 0:

```
correct += pred.eq(target.data).sum()
```

After summing the output of *.eq()* function, we will get a count of the number of times that the neural network produced the correct output, then we take an accumulating sum of the correct predictions to be able to determine the overall accuracy of our network on the test data. After we run through the test data in batches, we will print out the averaged accuracy and loss. This is shown below:

```
test_loss /= len(test_loader.dataset)
print('\nTest set: Average loss: {:.4f},
Accuracy: {}/{} ({:.0f}%)\n'.format(
        test_loss, correct,
len(test_loader.dataset),
        100. * correct /
len(test_loader.dataset)))
```

After training the network for a total of **10 epochs**, I got an accuracy of **97%**, which is not bad.

The complete code for the example should be as follows:

```
import torch
import torch.nn as nn
from torch.autograd import Variable
import torch.nn.functional as F
```

```python
from torchvision import datasets, transforms
import torch.optim as optim


def a_gradient():
    a = Variable(torch.ones(2, 2) * 2,
requires_grad=True)
    b = 2 * (a * a) + 5 * a
    # execute backpropagation
    b.backward(torch.ones(2, 2))
    print(a.grad)


def create_nnet(batch_size=200,
learning_rate=0.01, epochs=10,
                log_interval=10):


    train_loader =
torch.utils.data.DataLoader(
        datasets.MNIST('../data', train=True,
download=True,

transform=transforms.Compose([

transforms.ToTensor(),

transforms.Normalize((0.1307,), (0.3081,))
                    ])),
```

```
        batch_size=batch_size, shuffle=True)
    test_loader =
torch.utils.data.DataLoader(
        datasets.MNIST('../data',
train=False, transform=transforms.Compose([
            transforms.ToTensor(),
            transforms.Normalize((0.1307,),
(0.3081,))
        ])),
        batch_size=batch_size, shuffle=True)


    class NeuralNet(nn.Module):
        def __init__(self):
            super(NeuralNet, self).__init__()
            self.fc1 = nn.Linear(28 * 28,
200)
            self.fc2 = nn.Linear(200, 200)
            self.fc3 = nn.Linear(200, 10)

        def forward(self, x):
            x = F.relu(self.fc1(x))
            x = F.relu(self.fc2(x))
            x = self.fc3(x)
            return F.log_softmax(x)

    net = NeuralNet()
```

```python
print(net)

    # Lets first create a stochastic
gradient descent optimizer
    optimizer = optim.SGD(net.parameters(),
lr=learning_rate, momentum=0.9)
    # Then we create a loss function
    criterion = nn.NLLLoss()


    # execute the main training loop
    for epoch in range(epochs):
        for batch_idx, (data, target) in
enumerate(train_loader):
            data, target = Variable(data),
Variable(target)
            # resize the data from
(batch_size, 1, 28, 28) to (batch_size,
28*28)
            data = data.view(-1, 28*28)
            optimizer.zero_grad()
            n_out = net(data)
            loss = criterion(n_out, target)
            loss.backward()
            optimizer.step()
            if batch_idx % log_interval == 0:
```

```python
                print('Train Epoch: {} [{}/{}
({:.0f}%)]\tLoss: {:.6f}'.format(
                    epoch, batch_idx *
len(data), len(train_loader.dataset),
                        100. * batch_idx /
len(train_loader), loss.data))


    # Execute a test loop
    test_loss = 0
    correct = 0
    for data, target in test_loader:
        data, target = Variable(data,
volatile=True), Variable(target)
        data = data.view(-1, 28 * 28)
        net_out = net(data)
        # Get the sum of batch loss
        test_loss += criterion(n_out,
target).data
        pred = n_out.data.max(1)[1]  # get
the index of the max log-probability
        correct += pred.eq(target.data).sum()

    test_loss /= len(test_loader.dataset)
    print('\nTest set: Average loss: {:.4f},
Accuracy: {}/{} ({:.0f}%)\n'.format(
```

```
        test_loss, correct,
len(test_loader.dataset),
        100. * correct /
len(test_loader.dataset)))


if __name__ == "__main__":
    run_opt = 2
    if run_opt == 1:
        a_gradient()
    elif run_opt == 2:
        create_nnet()
```

Here is the last output from the code:

Chapter 9- Creating Convolutional Neural Networks with PyTorch

With a fully connected network with a few layers only, we cannot do much. When it comes to image processing, a lot of is needed. This means that more layers are needed in the network. However, we encounter a number of problems when we attempt to add more layers to a neural network. First, we risk facing the problem of vanishing gradient. However, we can solve this problem to some extend by using some sensible activation functions, like the **ReLU** family of activations. Another problem associated with a deep fully connected network is that the number of parameters that are trainable in the network, that is, the weights, can grow rapidly. This is an indication that the training may become practically impossible or slow down. The model will also be exposed to overfitting.

A convolutional neural network helps us solve the second problem above by exploiting the correlations between the adjacent inputs in images or the time series. Consider a situation in which we have images of cats and dogs. The pixels that are close to the eyes of the cat are more likely to be the same to the ones that are close to the cat's nose rather than those close to the dog's nose. What does this mean? It means that not every node in a layer needs to be connected to all other nodes in the next layer. This means that the number of weight parameters that need to be trained in the model will be cut. Convolutional neural networks also provide us with a number of tricks that make it easy for us to train the network.

These types of networks are used for classifying images, clustering them by similarity and for doing object recognition by scenes. These types of networks are capable of identifying faces, street signs, individuals, platypuses, eggplants, and other aspects regarding visual data.

They are used together with text analysis through the Optical Character Recognition **(OCR)** in which the images are seen as symbols which are to be transcribed and sound can be applied once they have been represented visually.

The use of neural networks in image recognition marks one of the reasons as to why deep learning has become so popular in the world. They are widely applied in fields such as machine visions which are highly used in robotics, self-driving cars, and treatments for visually impaired.

PyTorch is one of the deep learning frameworks suitable for the implementation of convolutional neural networks. We will be implementing one and use it to classify the MNIST digits.

Our input images will have **28 x 28 pixel greyscale** representations of digits. The first layer will be made up of **32** channels of **5 x 5 convolutional filters** plus a ReLU activation, which is followed by **2 x 2 max pooling** down-sampling with a stride of **2** (this will give a 14 x 14 output). In our next layer, we will have the **14 x 14** output of layer 1 under a scanning again and with **64 channels** of **5 x 5** convolutional filters plus a final **2 x 2** max pooling (**stride = 2**) down-sampling to generate a **7 x 7** output of layer **2**.

After the above stated convolutional part of our network, we will have a flatten operation that creates **7 x 7 x 64 = 3164** nodes, some intermediate layer of about **1000** fully connected nodes and a **softmax** operation over our 10 output nodes to generate some class probabilities. The layers will represent an output classifier.

Loading the Dataset

Since PyTorch comes with the **MNIST** dataset, we will simply load it via a DataLoader functionality. Let us first define the variables that we will need to use in the code:

```
# The hyperparameters
num_epochs = 5
num_classes = 10
batch_size = 100
```

```
learning_rate = 0.001
DATA_PATH = 'F:\\MNISTData'
MODEL_STORE_PATH = 'F:\\pytorch_models\\'
```

Those are the hyper parameters that we will need, so now they are setup. A specification of the drive in which we will be storing the MNIST dataset has also been specified as well as a storage location for the trained model hyper parameters after the completion of the training process.

We can now setup a transform that is to be applied to the MNIST dataset, as well as the dataset variables. This is shown below:

```
# transforms to apply to the data
trans =
transforms.Compose([transforms.ToTensor(),
transforms.Normalize((0.1307,), (0.3081,))])


# MNIST dataset
train_set =
torchvision.datasets.MNIST(root=DATA_PATH,
train=True, transform=trans, download=True)
test_set =
torchvision.datasets.MNIST(root=DATA_PATH,
train=False, transform=trans)
```

Note the use of ***transforms.Compose()*** function. The function comes from a torchvision package. It allows developers to setup various manipulations on a specified dataset. A number of transforms can be chained together in a list via the ***Compose()*** function. We first specified a transform that converts the input data set to a PyTorch tensor. The PyTorch tensor is simply a specific data type used in PyTorch for all different data and weight operations in the network.

In its simplest form, it is a multi-dimensional matrix. All the times, PyTorch expects the data set to be transformed into a tensor so that the data can be consumed by the network as the training and test set.

The next argument in our ***Compose()*** list is the normalization transformation. Neural networks perform better after the data has been normalized to range between -1 and **1** or **0** and **1**. For us to do this in PyTorch Normalize transform, we should supply the mean and standard deviation of MNIST dataset. In our case, the values for these are **0.1307** and **0.3081** respectively. For every input channel, one should supply a mean and a standard deviation. Our data, that is, MNIST, has only a single channel. If you have a dataset with more than one channel, then you must provide a mean and a standard deviation for each of the channels.

Next, we should create objects for ***train_dataset*** and ***test_dataset***. These will later be passed to data loader. For us to be able to create these two sets from the **MNIST** dataset, we have to pass in a number of arguments. First, we should have the *root* argument that specifies the folder in which ***train.pt*** and ***test.pt*** data files exist. The argument *train* is a Boolean that informs the data set to choose either the train.a pt data set or the **test.pt** data set. The next argument is ***transform,*** which is where we will be supplying any transform object that has been created to be applied to the data set, we will supply the *trans* object that was created earlier. We finally have the ***download*** argument that tells MNIST dataset function to download data from an online source if it is required.

Now that we have created both the train and test data sets, it is time for us to load them into our data loader. This can be done as follows:

```
train_loader = DataLoader(dataset=train_set,
batch_size=batch_size, shuffle=True)
test_loader = DataLoader(dataset=test_set,
batch_size=batch_size, shuffle=False)
```

In PyTorch, the data loader object provides us with a number of features that are useful in the consumption of training data, ability to shuffle our data easily, ability to batch data easily and make consumption of data much easily via the ability to employ multiprocessing to load the data quickly and easily. As shown above, there are three arguments that should be supplied, first being the data set that is to be loaded, second the batch size that you need and finally, you need to shuffle the data randomly. We can use the data loader as the iterator, so the standard python iterators like enumerate can be used for extraction of the data.

Building the Model

It is now time for us to setup the **nn**. Module class, which can be defined with the Convolutional Neural Network that we are about to train:

```python
class ConvNetwork(nn.Module):
    def __init__(self):
        super(ConvNetwork, self).__init__()
        self.layer1 = nn.Sequential(
            nn.Conv2d(1, 32, kernel_size=5,
stride=1, padding=2),
            nn.ReLU(),
            nn.MaxPool2d(kernel_size=2,
stride=2))
        self.layer2 = nn.Sequential(
```

```
        nn.Conv2d(32, 64, kernel_size=5,
stride=1, padding=2),
        nn.ReLU(),
        nn.MaxPool2d(kernel_size=2,
stride=2))
    self.drop_out = nn.Dropout()
    self.fc1 = nn.Linear(7 * 7 * 64,
1000)
    self.fc2 = nn.Linear(1000, 10)
```

We have defined our model. Anytime we need to create a structure in PyTorch, the simplest or basic way of doing it is by creating a class that inherits from the nn. Module super class. The nn.Module is a very useful class provided by PyTorch as it allows you to build deep learning networks. It also provides numerous methods like the ones for moving variables and performing operations on a GPU or CPU. We can also use it to apply recursive functions on all class properties and create streamlined interfaces to be used for training etc.

We should begin by creating a sequence of layer objects within the class _*init*_ function. We first create layer 1 via (*self.layer1*) by creating **nn.Sequential** object. The method will allow us to create some layers that are ordered sequentially in our network, and it is a great way of building a convolution + ReLU + pooling sequence.

As shown in our sequential definition, the first element is a **Conv2d nn.** *Module* method, which is a method for creating a set of convolutional filters. The first argument denotes the number of input channels, which in our case we have a single channel **grayscale** MNIST images, meaning the value of this argument will be 1. The second argument to the Conv2d should be the number of the output channels. The first convolutional filter layer has **32** channels, meaning that the value of our second argument will be **32**.

The argument ***kernel_size*** denotes the size of the convolutional filter, and in our case, we need **5** * **5** sized convolutional filters, meaning that the value of this argument will be **5**. If you need filters with different sized shapes in x and y directions, you should supply (**x-size, y-size**). Finally, you should specify the padding argument. This takes a bit complex thought. The output size of any dimension from a pooling operation or convolutional filtering can be computed using the formula given below:

$$W_{out} = \frac{(W_{in} - F + 2P)}{S} + 1$$

The W_{in} denotes the width of the output, F denotes the filter size, P denotes the padding while S denotes the stride. The same formula should be applied in the calculation of the height, but since our image and filtering are symmetrical, the same formula can be applied to both. If there is a need to keep both the input and output dimensions the same, with a stride of **1** and a filter of **5**, then from the above formula, we will need padding of **2**. This means that the value of padding argument in **Conv2d** is **2**.

The next element in our sequence is a **ReLU** activation. The last element to be added to the sequential definition of **_self.layer1_** is max pooling operation. The first argument should be the pooling size, **2 * 2**, meaning that the argument will have a value of **2**. Secondly, we should down-sample the data by reducing the effective size of the image by a factor of **2**. For this to be done with the above formula, the stride should be set to **2**, and the padding to **0**. This means that the stride argument should be equal to 2. The padding argument has a default value of **0** if it is not specified, and this is what has been done in the above code. From such calculations, it is clear that the output of **_self.layer1_** will be **32** channels of the **14 * 14** images.

The second layer, that is, **_self.layer2_**, has been defined in the same way as the first layer. The difference is that the input to the **Conv2d** function has **32** channels, and an output of **64** channels. By use of the same logic and knowing the pooling down-sampling, the *self.layer2* should give an output of 64 channels of **7 * 7** images.

Next, we should specify a drop-out layer to avoid the problem of overfitting in the model. Finally, we have to create two fully connected layers. The first layer will have a size of **7 x 7 x 64** nodes which will be connected to the second layer of **1000 nodes**. Anytime you need to create a fully connected layer in PyTorch, you should use the **nn.Linear method**. The first argument to the method should be the number of nodes to the layer, while the second argument should be the number of nodes in the following layer.

With the definition of **_init_**, the definitions of the layers have been created. We should now define the way the data flows through the network layers when performing the forward pass:

```python
def forward(self, y):
    out = self.layer1(y)
    out = self.layer2(out)
    out = out.reshape(out.size(0), -1)
    out = self.drop_out(out)
```

```
out = self.fc1(out)
out = self.fc2(out)
return out
```

It is of importance for us to give this method the name *forward* as it will override the base forward function in the nn. Module and allow all **nn**. Module functionality to work in the right way. As you can see, an input argument y is required, which is data to be passed to the model, that is, a batch of data. This data is passed to the first layer, that is, *self.layer1* and the returned output is *out*. The output is passed to the next layer in the sequence and this process continues. After the *self-layer2*, a reshaping function is applied to the *out*, and the data dimensions will be flattened from **7 x 7 x 64** into **3164 x 1**. The dropout will be applied next followed by two fully connected layers, and the final output will be returned from this function.

At this point, we have defined the architecture of our convolutional neural network, so it is time to train it.

Training the Model

Before we can begin to train the network, let us first create an instance of our class, that is, **ConvNetwork class**, and then define the loss function and the optimizer.

```
mod = ConvNetwork()
```

```
# Loss and the optimizer
criterion = nn.CrossEntropyLoss()
optimizer =
torch.optim.Adam(model.parameters(),
lr=learning_rate)
```

First, we have created an instance of the ConvNetwork class and given it the name **mod**. We have then defined the loss operation that we are going to use for calculation of the loss. We have used the **CrossEntropyLoss()** function provided by PyTorch. Note that we have not defined SoftMax activation for our final classification layer. This is the reason because the **CrossEntropyLoss()** function comes with a combination of SoftMax and cross entropy loss function in one function. This means that when we use the CrossEntropyLoss() function, we have used these two function.

Next, we have defined an Adam optimizer. The first argument to this optimizer are the parameters that we need the optimizer to train. This has been made simply by the nn. Module class that the ConvNetwork derives from. We only have to pass **model.parameters()** to the function then PyTorch will keep track of all the parameters which need to be trained within the model. We have finally supplied the learning rate.

Let us now create the training loop:

```python
# Training the model
steps = len(train_loader)
loss_list = []
acc_list = []
for epoch in range(total_epochs):
    for a, (images, labels) in
enumerate(train_loader):
        # Running a forward pass
        result = model(images)
        loss = criterion(result, labels)
        loss_list.append(loss.item())

        # Backprop then perform an Adam
optimization
        optimizer.zero_grad()
        loss.backward()
        optimizer.step()

        # For tracking the accuracy
        total = labels.size(0)
        _, predicted = torch.max(result.data,
1)
        correct = (predicted ==
labels).sum().item()
```

```
acc_list.append(correct / total)

if (a + 1) % 100 == 0:
    print('Epoch [{}/{}], Step
[{}/{}], Loss: {:.4f}, Accuracy: {:.2f}%'
            .format(epoch + 1,
total_epochs, a + 1, steps, loss.item(),
                    (correct / total) *
100))
```

The important parts in the above code are the ones that
begin with loops. First, we have looped over the number of
epochs, and within the loop, we have iterated over
train_loader using enumerate. Within the inner loop, we
have first calculated the outputs of the forward pass. This has
been done by passing the images to it. The images are simply
a batch of MNIST images from the ***train_loader*** and they
have been normalized. Note that we should not call the
model.forward(images) since the nn.Module knows that
the ***forward*** should be called when it executes the
model(images).
In the next step, we should pass the outputs of the model and
the true image labels to the CrossEntropyLoss function,
which is defined as the *criterion*. The loss has been appended
to a list that will later be used to plot the training progress. In

the step, we should perform a back-propagation and optimized training step. First, the gradients have to be zero, which can be achieved by calling **zero_grad()** on the optimizer. Next, we have to call the **.backward()** on the loss variable to do a back-propagation. After calculating the gradients on the back-propagation, we have to call the **optimizer.step()** to perform Adam optimizer training step. With PyTorch, training of the model becomes very easy and intuitive.

In the next steps, we should be focused on keeping track of the accuracy on the training set. We can determine the model predictions using the **torch.max()** function, which will return the index of the maximum value in the tensor. The function's first argument is the tensor that is to be examined, while the second argument to the function is the axis over which we need to determine the index of the maximum. The model will give an output sensor of size size (batch_size, 10). To determine the prediction of the model, for every sample in the batch, we should find the maximum value of our 10 output nodes. Each of these will be corresponding to one of MNIST handwritten digits, that is, output 2 will correspond to digit "2" and this continues. The output node that has the highest value will be the prediction of the model. This means that we should the second argument of the **torch.max()** function to a 1, which points to the maximum function to examine output node axis. An **axis=0** will be corresponding to the dimension of the batch size.

This will return a list of prediction integers from our model, with the next line comparing the predictions to the true labels *(predicted == labels)* then gets their sum to know the number of correct predictions. Note that the output from the *sum()* will still be a tensor, so for you to be able to access its value, you should call *.item()*. The number of correct predictions should be divided by the batch_size, which is the same as *labels.size(0)*, to get the accuracy.

Finally, during the process of training and after every **100 iterations** of the inner loop, the progress will be printed.

Model Testing

We now need to test our model and see how accurate it is. The testing will be done using the test dataset. Here is the code for this task:

```
# Model testing
mod.eval()
with torch.no_grad():
    correct = 0
    total = 0
    for images, labels in test_loader:
        result = model(images)
```

```
        _, predicted = torch.max(result.data,
1)
        total += labels.size(0)
        correct += (predicted ==
labels).sum().item()

    print('The model's Test Accuracy: {}
%'.format((correct / total) * 100))


torch.save(mod.state_dict(), MODEL_STORE_PATH
+ 'conv_network_model.ckpt')
```

The model was first set to an evaluation mode by running **_mod.eval()_**. This function is handy and it disables any drop-out or batch normalization layers in the model, and it has the effect of befuddling your model testing/evaluation, which will have the effect of speeding up the computations. The rest of it is similar to the computation of the accuracy during training, with the exception being that the code will iterate through **the _test_loader_**.

The result has been sent to the console and the **_torch.save()_** function has been called to save the model.

At this point, you should have the following code:

```python
import torch
import torch.nn as nn
import torchvision.transforms as transforms
from torch.utils.data import DataLoader
import numpy as np
import torchvision.datasets

# The hyperparameters
total_epochs = 5
num_classes = 10
batch_size = 100
learning_rate = 0.001

DATA_PATH = 'F:\\MNISTData'
MODEL_STORE_PATH = 'F:\\pytorch_models\\'

# data transforms to be applied
trans =
transforms.Compose([transforms.ToTensor(),
transforms.Normalize((0.1307,), (0.3081,))])

# the MNIST dataset
```

```python
train_set =
torchvision.datasets.MNIST(root=DATA_PATH,
train=True, transform=trans, download=True)
test_set =
torchvision.datasets.MNIST(root=DATA_PATH,
train=False, transform=trans)

train_loader = DataLoader(dataset=train_set,
batch_size=batch_size, shuffle=True)
test_loader = DataLoader(dataset=test_set,
batch_size=batch_size, shuffle=False)

# Convolutional neural network (two
convolutional layers)
class ConvNetwork(nn.Module):
    def __init__(self):
        super(ConvNetwork, self).__init__()
        self.layer1 = nn.Sequential(
            nn.Conv2d(1, 32, kernel_size=5,
stride=1, padding=2),
            nn.ReLU(),
            nn.MaxPool2d(kernel_size=2,
stride=2))
        self.layer2 = nn.Sequential(
            nn.Conv2d(32, 64, kernel_size=5,
stride=1, padding=2),
```

```
            nn.ReLU(),
            nn.MaxPool2d(kernel_size=2,
stride=2))
        self.drop_out = nn.Dropout()
        self.fc1 = nn.Linear(7 * 7 * 64,
1000)
        self.fc2 = nn.Linear(1000, 10)

    def forward(self, x):
        out = self.layer1(x)
        out = self.layer2(out)
        out = out.reshape(out.size(0), -1)
        out = self.drop_out(out)
        out = self.fc1(out)
        out = self.fc2(out)
        return out


model = ConvNetwork()

# Loss and optimizer
criterion = nn.CrossEntropyLoss()
optimizer =
torch.optim.Adam(model.parameters(),
lr=learning_rate)
```

```python
# Training the model
total_step = len(train_loader)
loss_list = []
acc_list = []
for epoch in range(total_epochs):
    for i, (images, labels) in enumerate(train_loader):
        # Run a forward pass
        outputs = model(images)
        loss = criterion(outputs, labels)
        loss_list.append(loss.item())

        # Backprop then perform an Adam optimization
        optimizer.zero_grad()
        loss.backward()
        optimizer.step()

        # Tracking accuracy
        total = labels.size(0)
        _, predicted = torch.max(outputs.data, 1)
        correct = (predicted == labels).sum().item()
        acc_list.append(correct / total)
```

```python
        if (i + 1) % 100 == 0:
            print('Epoch [{}/{}], Step
[{}/{}], Loss: {:.4f}, Accuracy: {:.2f}%'
                    .format(epoch + 1,
total_epochs, i + 1, total_step, loss.item(),
                            (correct / total) *
100))


# Model testing
model.eval()
with torch.no_grad():
    correct = 0
    total = 0
    for images, labels in test_loader:
        outputs = model(images)
        _, predicted =
torch.max(outputs.data, 1)
        total += labels.size(0)
        correct += (predicted ==
labels).sum().item()


    print('Test Accuracy of the model on the
10000 test images: {} %'.format((correct /
total) * 100))


# Saving model and create a plot
```

```
torch.save(model.state_dict(),
MODEL_STORE_PATH + 'conv_network_model.ckpt')
```

The code returns the following output upon execution:

```
Epoch [1/5], Step [100/600], Loss: 0.2146, Accuracy: 95.00%
Epoch [1/5], Step [200/600], Loss: 0.0860, Accuracy: 96.00%
Epoch [1/5], Step [300/600], Loss: 0.2204, Accuracy: 92.00%
Epoch [1/5], Step [400/600], Loss: 0.1295, Accuracy: 95.00%
Epoch [1/5], Step [500/600], Loss: 0.0789, Accuracy: 97.00%
Epoch [1/5], Step [600/600], Loss: 0.0700, Accuracy: 96.00%
Epoch [2/5], Step [100/600], Loss: 0.1221, Accuracy: 96.00%
Epoch [2/5], Step [200/600], Loss: 0.0859, Accuracy: 95.00%
Epoch [2/5], Step [300/600], Loss: 0.0460, Accuracy: 100.00%
Epoch [2/5], Step [400/600], Loss: 0.0646, Accuracy: 99.00%
Epoch [2/5], Step [500/600], Loss: 0.1899, Accuracy: 94.00%
Epoch [2/5], Step [600/600], Loss: 0.1850, Accuracy: 94.00%
Epoch [3/5], Step [100/600], Loss: 0.0506, Accuracy: 98.00%
Epoch [3/5], Step [200/600], Loss: 0.0656, Accuracy: 98.00%
Epoch [3/5], Step [300/600], Loss: 0.0296, Accuracy: 99.00%
Epoch [3/5], Step [400/600], Loss: 0.1290, Accuracy: 97.00%
Epoch [3/5], Step [500/600], Loss: 0.0683, Accuracy: 99.00%
Epoch [3/5], Step [600/600], Loss: 0.0384, Accuracy: 98.00%
Epoch [4/5], Step [100/600], Loss: 0.1422, Accuracy: 98.00%
Epoch [4/5], Step [200/600], Loss: 0.0621, Accuracy: 98.00%
Epoch [4/5], Step [300/600], Loss: 0.0237, Accuracy: 98.00%
Epoch [4/5], Step [400/600], Loss: 0.1210, Accuracy: 96.00%
Epoch [4/5], Step [500/600], Loss: 0.0686, Accuracy: 98.00%
Epoch [4/5], Step [600/600], Loss: 0.1129, Accuracy: 98.00%
Epoch [5/5], Step [100/600], Loss: 0.1042, Accuracy: 96.00%
Epoch [5/5], Step [200/600], Loss: 0.0819, Accuracy: 98.00%
Epoch [5/5], Step [300/600], Loss: 0.0963, Accuracy: 96.00%
Epoch [5/5], Step [400/600], Loss: 0.1165, Accuracy: 97.00%
Epoch [5/5], Step [500/600], Loss: 0.0717, Accuracy: 98.00%
Epoch [5/5], Step [600/600], Loss: 0.0492, Accuracy: 99.00%
Test Accuracy of the model on the 10000 test images: 99.00999999999999 %
```

The model has returned an accuracy of **99.01%** on the **1000** test images. This shows that the model gave a very high degree of accuracy on the training set, and after 6 epochs, the accuracy of the test set reaches **99%**, which is not bad. This accuracy is a bit high than what we achieved with the fully connected network, in which we had achieved an accuracy of **98%**.

Chapter 10- Creating Recurrent Neural Networks with PyTorch

These are a type of neural network which has designed so as to recognize patterns obtained from sequences of data such as text, handwriting, gnomes, spoken word, or the numerical time series data which might be coming from government agencies, stock markets, and sensors.

These form the most powerful form of neural networks which can be applied to objects such as images and break them up so as to get continuous patches of data and the patches will be treated as a sequence. The recurrent neural networks have a memory which resembles the human brain.

In this type of network, the input is received, and not only the current input but also the previous input which they had received. Note that the decision which a current network reaches at time t-1 usually affects the decision which is attained at time t. This means that the current decision is determined on the previous decision. That is why we use the term **"recurrent"** to describe these types of networks. This means that recurrent networks usually have two sources of input, one being the current input and the other one being the previous decision. When these two are combined, the neural network decides on how to respond to the data.

The infinite loop usually differentiates the recurrent networks from the **feedforward networks**. It is believed that the recurrent networks have a memory, and this memory makes the recurrent networks able to perform the tasks which the feedforward networks are unable to perform.

The sequential information for this type of network is hidden in its hidden state. We need to create sequence and demonstrate how to create and use a recurrent neural network with PyTorch. The input sequence will be made up of 20 data points, with the target sequence being the same as the input sequence.

Let us first import all the packages that are necessary for us to implement a recurrent neural network:

```
import torch
import torch.nn.init as init
import numpy as np
from torch.autograd import Variable
import pylab as pl
```

Note that you will get the pylab module after installing matplotlib.

It is now time for us to set the **hyperparmeters** for our model. The input layer will have a size of **7. 1** input neuron and **6** context neurons will be used for the purpose of creating the target sequence. This can be done as follows:

```
dtype = torch.FloatTensor
input_size, hidden_size, output_size = 7, 6,
1
epochs = 250
sequence_length = 20
lr = 0.1
data_steps = np.linspace(2, 10,
sequence_length + 1)
data = np.sin(data_steps)
data.resize((sequence_length + 1, 1))

x = Variable(torch.Tensor(data[:-
1]).type(dtype), requires_grad=False)
y =
Variable(torch.Tensor(data[1:]).type(dtype),
requires_grad=False)
```

The above code will help us to generate the training data, in which **x** will be the input data while y is the required target sequence.

It is now time for us to initialize the weights for our network. We will use a normal distribution and a mean of zero. **W1** will be used to represent the acceptance of input variables while **w2** will be representing the output generated as follows:

```
w1 = torch.FloatTensor(input_size,
hidden_size).type(dtype)
init.normal(w1, 0.0, 0.4)
w1 = Variable(w1, requires_grad = True)
w2 = torch.FloatTensor(hidden_size,
output_size).type(dtype)
init.normal(w2, 0.0, 0.3)
w2 = Variable(w2, requires_grad = True)
```

We can now define a feed forward function. This function will help us to define a unique neural network.

Here is the code for the function:

```
def forwardFunc(input, cont_state, w1, w2):
    xh = torch.cat((input, cont_state), 1)
    cont_state = torch.tanh(xh.mm(w1))
    out = cont_state.mm(w2)
    return (out, cont_state)
```

We can now begin to train the sine wave implementation of the recurrent neural network. The outer loop will iterate over every loop while the inner loop will be iterating over the elements of our sequence. We will be calculating the Mean Square Error (MSE) which we will use to predict the continuous variables. This is shown below:

```
for i in range(total_epochs):
    total_loss = 0
    cont_state = Variable(torch.zeros((1,
hidden_size)).type(dtype), requires_grad =
True)
    for j in range(x.size(0)):
        input = x[j:(j+1)]
        target = y[j:(j+1)]
        (pred, cont_state) = forwardFunc(input,
cont_state, w1, w2)
        loss = (pred - target).pow(2).sum()/2
        total_loss += loss
        loss.backward()
        w1.data -= lr * w1.grad.data
        w2.data -= lr * w2.grad.data
        w1.grad.data.zero_()
        w2.grad.data.zero_()
        cont_state = Variable(cont_state.data)
    if i % 10 == 0:
        print("Epoch: {} loss {}".format(i,
total_loss.data[0]))
```

```
cont_state = Variable(torch.zeros((1,
hidden_size)).type(dtype), requires_grad =
False)
predictions = []


for i in range(x.size(0)):
    input = x[i:i+1]
    (pred, cont_state) = forwardFunc(input,
cont_state, w1, w2)
    cont_state = cont_state


predictions.append(pred.data.numpy().ravel()[
0])
```

We can now create a plot of sine wave as it is required. Here is the code for this:

```
pl.scatter(data_time_steps[:-1],
x.data.numpy(), s = 90, label = "Actual")
pl.scatter(data_time_steps[1:], predictions,
label = "Predicted")
pl.legend()
pl.show()
```

You are then done. You should now have the following as the complete code:

```python
import torch
import torch.nn.init as init
import numpy as np
from torch.autograd import Variable
import pylab as pl
dtype = torch.FloatTensor
input_size, hidden_size, output_size = 7, 6,
1
total_epochs = 250
sequence_length = 20
lr = 0.1
data_steps = np.linspace(2, 10,
sequence_length + 1)
data = np.sin(data_steps)
data.resize((sequence_length + 1, 1))
x = Variable(torch.Tensor(data[:-
1]).type(dtype), requires_grad=False)
y =
Variable(torch.Tensor(data[1:]).type(dtype),
requires_grad=False)
w1 = torch.FloatTensor(input_size,
hidden_size).type(dtype)
init.normal(w1, 0.0, 0.4)
```

```
w1 = Variable(w1, requires_grad = True)
w2 = torch.FloatTensor(hidden_size,
output_size).type(dtype)
init.normal(w2, 0.0, 0.3)
w2 = Variable(w2, requires_grad = True)


def forwardFunc(input, cont_state, w1, w2):
    xh = torch.cat((input, cont_state), 1)
    cont_state = torch.tanh(xh.mm(w1))
    out = cont_state.mm(w2)
    return (out, cont_state)


for i in range(total_epochs):
    total_loss = 0
    cont_state = Variable(torch.zeros((1,
hidden_size)).type(dtype), requires_grad =
True)
    for j in range(x.size(0)):
        input = x[j:(j+1)]
        target = y[j:(j+1)]
        (pred, cont_state) = forwardFunc(input,
cont_state, w1, w2)
        loss = (pred - target).pow(2).sum()/2
        total_loss += loss
        loss.backward()
        w1.data -= lr * w1.grad.data
```

```
      w2.data -= lr * w2.grad.data
      w1.grad.data.zero_()
      w2.grad.data.zero_()
      cont_state = Variable(cont_state.data)
   if i % 10 == 0:
      print("Epoch: {} loss {}".format(i,
total_loss.data[0]))
cont_state = Variable(torch.zeros((1,
hidden_size)).type(dtype), requires_grad =
False)
predictions = []


for i in range(x.size(0)):
   input = x[i:i+1]
   (pred, cont_state) = forwardFunc(input,
cont_state, w1, w2)
   cont_state = cont_state


predictions.append(pred.data.numpy().ravel()[
0])


pl.scatter(data_steps[:-1], x.data.numpy(), s
= 90, label = "Actual")
pl.scatter(data_steps[1:], predictions, label
= "Predicted")
pl.legend()
```

You can now execute your code. You will see the progress of execution in which you will see the number of the epoch and the amount of loss.

This is shown below:

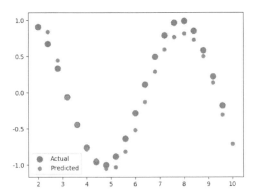

```
Epoch: 0 loss 3.8820152282714844
Epoch: 10 loss 0.12618400156497955
Epoch: 20 loss 0.10419636964797974
Epoch: 30 loss 0.09071795642375946
Epoch: 40 loss 0.08038729429244995
Epoch: 50 loss 0.07019225507974625
Epoch: 60 loss 0.05802913382649422
Epoch: 70 loss 0.04187462478876114
Epoch: 80 loss 0.02230309508740902
Epoch: 90 loss 0.04074844345450401
Epoch: 100 loss 0.08864261209964752
Epoch: 110 loss 0.10393358021974564
Epoch: 120 loss 0.10996054857969284
Epoch: 130 loss 0.1133623942732811
Epoch: 140 loss 0.11544793099164963
Epoch: 150 loss 0.11656742542982101
Epoch: 160 loss 0.11685743927955627
Epoch: 170 loss 0.11638361215591143
Epoch: 180 loss 0.11518278717994698
Epoch: 190 loss 0.11328156292438507
Epoch: 200 loss 0.11071975529193878
Epoch: 210 loss 0.10754640400409698
Epoch: 220 loss 0.10382597148418427
Epoch: 230 loss 0.09964451193889509
Epoch: 240 loss 0.09509380161762238
```

As the output shows, the amount of loss reduces after each epoch. The generated scatter plot is as shown below:

You have created a neural network, trained it and obtained the results.

Conclusion

This marks the end of this guide. Deep learning is a great technique for processing huge amounts of data. That is why it is mostly used for processing datasets involving images. Deep learning involves the creation of artificial neural networks. These are machine learning models that operate based on how the human mind work. These models can be used for extracting patterns, trends and relations between various variables in a dataset. They can also be used for calculating a number of statistical measures from datasets. Businesses with such information can enjoy a competitive advantage over those without. The reason is that this information is very rich and it can be used for making sound decisions as far as running the business is concerned. Python is a good programming language for building such machine learning models. There are many Python libraries that can be used for this. In this book, we have discussed TensorFlow, Keras and PyTorch.

Others books from the same collection by Samuel Burns

Printed in Great Britain
by Amazon

40735902R00097